IPOs and Entrepreneurial Firms

IPOs and Entrepreneurial Firms

Giancarlo Giudici
School of Management Politecnico di Milano
Italy
giancarlo.giudici@polimi.it

Silvio Vismara
Department of Management
University of Bergamo
Italy
silvio.vismara@unibg.it

the essence of knowledge
Boston — Delft

Foundations and Trends® in Entrepreneurship

Published, sold and distributed by:
now Publishers Inc.
PO Box 1024
Hanover, MA 02339
United States
Tel. +1-781-985-4510
www.nowpublishers.com
sales@nowpublishers.com

Outside North America:
now Publishers Inc.
PO Box 179
2600 AD Delft
The Netherlands
Tel. +31-6-51115274

The preferred citation for this publication is

G. Giudici and S. Vismara. *IPOs and Entrepreneurial Firms.* Foundations and Trends® in Entrepreneurship, vol. 17, no. 8, pp. 766–852, 2021.

ISBN: 978-1-68083-868-8
© 2021 G. Giudici and S. Vismara

Foundations and Trends® in Entrepreneurship
Volume 17, Issue 8, 2021
Editorial Board

Editorial Scope

Topics

Foundations and Trends® in Entrepreneurship publishes survey and tutorial articles in the following topics:

- Nascent and start-up entrepreneurs
- Opportunity recognition
- New venture creation process
- Business formation
- Firm ownership
- Market value and firm growth
- Franchising
- Managerial characteristics and behavior of entrepreneurs
- Strategic alliances and networks
- Government programs and public policy
- Gender and ethnicity

- New business financing:
  - Business angels
  - Bank financing, debt, and trade credit
  - Venture capital and private equity capital
  - Public equity and IPOs
- Family-owned firms
- Management structure, governance and performance
- Corporate entrepreneurship
- High technology:
  - Technology-based new firms
  - High-tech clusters
- Small business and economic growth

Information for Librarians

Foundations and Trends® in Entrepreneurship, 2021, Volume 17, 4 issues. ISSN paper version 1551-3114. ISSN online version 1551-3122. Also available as a combined paper and online subscription.

Contents

1   Introduction   3

2   The Going Public Decision   7

3   Pricing and Valuation   25

4   Intermediaries in the IPO Process   35

5   Short- and Long-Run Performance   43
    5.1   Underpricing   45
    5.2   Long-Run Underperformance   48

6   Trends in the Number of IPOs   67

7   Directions and Trends   71

References   75

IPOs and Entrepreneurial Firms

Giancarlo Giudici[1] and Silvio Vismara[2]

[1]School of Management Politecnico di Milano, Italy;
giancarlo.giudici@polimi.it
[2]Department of Management, University of Bergamo, Italy;
silvio.vismara@unibg.it

ABSTRACT

The listing on a stock exchange is a paramount milestone
in the life cycle of an enterprise. By taking their company
public on a stock market through an Initial Public Offering
(IPO), entrepreneurs may target several benefits (e.g., raising money, facilitating acquisitions, offering valuable stock
ownership plans to employees) but their firms will bear new
costs and requirements. In this work we review the academic
literature on IPOs of entrepreneurial firms, focusing on five
main topics: (i) the going public decision, (ii) pricing and
valuation, (iii) the role of intermediaries and underwriters
in the listing process, (iv) the performance of IPO-firms in
the short and long run, and (v) market cycles in the IPO
industry.

Giancarlo Giudici and Silvio Vismara (2021), "IPOs and Entrepreneurial Firms",
Foundations and Trends® in Entrepreneurship: Vol. 17, No. 8, pp 766–852. DOI:
10.1561/0300000067.

1

Introduction

An initial public offering (IPO) allows a privately held company to raise capital by offering equity stock to the general public. Companies involved in IPOs are aware of the potential benefits. The money raised may increase its growth capital. The entrepreneurs obtain an objective valuation of their company. On the other side, the status of a listed company increases public exposure and is associated with increased costs and requirements.

The first IPO in the United States was in 1783 when Bank of America went public by selling shares of stock. In Europe, the Dutch East India Company issued public shares in 1602 to raise capital to fund the expansion of its operations. Notwithstanding more than 400 years passed away, taking a company public holds a special place in entrepreneurs' (and investors') imagination. IPOs are glorious and well-publicized. They certify that a company did not fail and may continue to grow autonomously, with thousands of shareholders trading the stock and new wealth created.

In this monograph, we propose an analysis of the most recent literature on IPOs of entrepreneurial firms, focusing on the contributions published mainly in entrepreneurship and finance journals. We refer to entrepreneurial firms as young firms, based on intangible rather than physical assets, where the founder of the firm often serves as the key inventor and the CEO. Although taking an entrepreneurial perspective, a contribution of this monograph is to bring together different streams of literature. Entrepreneurial finance literature is indeed largely segmented (Cumming and Vismara, 2017). Different streams of the academic literature between entrepreneurship and finance have become segmented for reasons of theoretical tractability and data availability. The literature on entrepreneurial finance has evolved through distinct paths, with the same topic often being addressed from multiple perspectives. When different streams of research study the same thing, authors might respond by conveniently ignoring work by other authors, to make their studies look innovative to a segmented readership. In this monograph, we aim at contributing to reducing this gap by highlighting topics that have been widely investigated by scholars as well as pointing out themes that are still relatively uncovered.

The subject of the monograph, IPOs and entrepreneurial firms, covers a very broad area of topics. The richness of the literature spanning from finance to management journals forces us to make some choices. While many aspects of the IPO process are of interest and many theoretical advancements have been put forward, this study is necessarily focused on a few ones. For sake of focus, we did not consider relevant aspects such as the role of financial intermediaries or the role of the policies and regulation. We do consider IPO performance but only in terms of short-term or long-term share price and operating performance, paying little attention to other measures such as the survival of IPO firms. A broader range of topics are discussed in previous works on IPOs, such as Levis and Vismara (2013) or Lowry *et al.* (2017).

Both IPOs and entrepreneurial ventures vary across "space and time". This survey is less focused on the context but more on general findings which, we acknowledge, could not necessarily be generalized or treated as stylized facts. A clear example comes from the valuation of firms going public. To satisfy investors' demand for reliable valuation guidelines, scholars have highlighted several interesting "stylized facts," mainly related to the valuation of IPOs. For instance, existing studies find that the skills and abilities of entrepreneurial teams, along with affiliation with prestigious third parties, are effective signals of firm quality, leading to higher valuation (e.g., Bruton *et al.*, 2009; Sanders and Boivie, 2004). However, the fragmented nature of this evidence prevents it from providing reliable theory-based guidelines for investors, either professional or retail. In particular, whether this evidence can be extended to other financial milestones, such as private deals or equity crowdfunding offerings (Block *et al.*, 2018), is debatable.

The structure of this work is as follows. In Section 2 we review the literature on the reasons why companies go public. A trade-off between direct and indirect costs and benefits is considered, as well as entrepreneurial strategic objectives, comprising engaging more easily in acquisitions, signaling the quality of the company, increasing its reputation. Section 3 deals with alternative methodologies to price IPO shares, including cash flow discounting and peer comparison. Section 4 describes the role of intermediaries in the placement of IPO shares. Section 5 focuses on the short-run (underpricing) and long-run performance of IPO companies. Section 6 discusses the cyclical dynamics of the IPO flow on the market. Finally, in Section 7 we identify future research directions at the cross-road between finance and entrepreneurship and comparing IPOs with new digital finance, with the hope to help de-segmenting research and provide new ideas.

2

The Going Public Decision

This section examines the recent evolution of IPOs and concentrates on the study of the factors motivating and inducing companies to go public. Although this is not a new argument in the scientific literature, new theoretical ideas and new empirical evidence are presented. The generic perspective taken is to investigate the decision to go public by analyzing the costs and benefits from both the point of view of the company (opportunity to raise capital to finance company growth, reduce outstanding liabilities, improve image) and from that of its shareholders (liquidity, portfolio diversification, the disclosure of a price for the shares). Therefore, the first question requiring answers is the following: why do companies decide to go public?

For decades the answer to this question has been sought in the literature and numerous articles have recently been published on the subject. A plethora of study methods is possible, with the most relevant and up-to-date being explored in this section. In particular, three main reasons for the decision of the firm to launch an IPO can be distinguished:

(a) the opportunity to raise new capital and obtain other financial benefits;

(b) the company's image and reputation improve;

(c) the existing shareholders' benefit.

The literature makes an important contribution in identifying the reasons underlying the decision to go public and interpreting them in terms of the financial structure of the company. In fact, the IPO is an extraordinary financial operation that represents an opportunity for the company to improve its liquidity through raising funds from new shareholders and consequently change its financial structure. Therefore, the decision to go public can be viewed as a result of financial policy and forms part of a wider debate on defining the optimal financial structure for the company. Modigliani and Miller (1958) demonstrated how the financial structure of the company is irrelevant compared to maximizing value in suitable cases. Nevertheless, reality shows how an increase in leverage over and above a certain level increases the risk of bankruptcy, resulting in the so-called "costs of financial distress". Consequently, not only the benefits but also the costs of every possible source of financing need to be taken into consideration, which results in the fundamental conclusion of "trade-off theories" being fulfilled. According to these theories, companies choose the most suitable type of financing by optimizing the cost/benefit trade-off. The benefits are enjoyed by both shareholders and the company, and for the latter, they can refer to both its managerial and financial functions.

Among the financial benefits to the company, there is, firstly, access to new sources of financing to fund growth. This "noble" reason appears in the great majority of prospectuses (excepting those for privatization) as the main reason behind the offering (Ellingsen and Rydqvist, 1997; Rydqvist and Högholm, 1995). When internally generated cash flow is insufficient, the stock markets offer the opportunity to tap into financial sources without the mediation of financial intermediaries such as banks or venture capital (VC) (Holmström and Tirole, 1993). The capital raised at the IPO allows companies to grow by extraordinary financial operations such as mergers, acquisitions, and joint-ventures (Planell, 1995). This seems to happen frequently with high tech companies which often invest the funds obtained via the IPO in external rather than internal growth (Schultz and Zaman, 2001). Reasons for this include technological opportunities as in some sectors it is particularly important to reach "critical mass" in terms of market share. Consequently, the flotation is an opportunity to raise precious capital to achieve company growth objectives otherwise limited by financial constraints (Carpenter and Petersen, 2002). At the same time, *ceteris paribus*, the equity capital raised through the issuance of primary shares reduces the leverage ratio.

Small and medium-sized enterprises (SMEs) are recognized worldwide as a key source of dynamism, innovation and flexibility in advanced industrialized countries, as well as in emerging and developing economies. However, the financing patterns for SMEs hint at the presence of greater constraints than those borne by large companies. Such financing constraints mean that there are significant numbers of SMEs that could use funds productively, were they available.

The level of information asymmetry between a firm and its external investors is typically higher for SMEs than for large companies. First, information on small enterprises, especially those not publicly traded, is often limited and less timely. Second, reduced bargaining power with financiers and the presence of fixed costs in financing activity both make external finance more expensive for SMEs. Third, information asymmetries are particularly severe for high-tech SMEs, given the valuation difficulties of intangible assets. The cost of bankruptcy is larger for smaller firms, and intangible assets are difficult to serve as collateral. These two factors also tend to dissuade external sources of financing.

These arguments suggest that SMEs should exhibit a greater reliance on internally generated funds (such as personal funds). Thus, SMEs may suffer from a lack of alternative financing sources. Innovative SMEs in particular undertake risky projects and have mostly intangible assets, making debt financing unsuitable. Debt holders bear the downside risk, but do not share the upside benefit of successful innovation. Much of the research and policy discussion on high-tech SMEs therefore revolves around the unsuitability of debt and the merits of equity for external early-stage financing. Thus, for many entrepreneurial ventures, an IPO enables management to pursue growth opportunities that would otherwise be impossible to fund and allows the reallocation of productive resources from non-surviving to surviving high-tech firms (Audretsch and Lehmann, 2008). On the other hand, stock exchanges are generally open to retail unsophisticated investors, who need to be protected and warned against the risk of investing in risky IPO companies. Costs of compliance and investor-relator offices are relevant and hardly sustainable for startups and SMEs.

To this extent, regulators and exchanges allowed the establishment of junior unregulated segments of the stock market, to create an adequate "seasoning" setting with less tight requirements and lower admission fees. Vismara *et al.* (2012) explored the second-tier exchanges around Europe. They point out three different models: (i) second-tier markets for SMEs destined to "feed" first-tier exchanges, (ii) sectorial markets (e.g., for technology companies), and (iii) "demand-side" unregulated segments.

In their book, Giudici and Roosenboom (2004) analyzed "new" exchanges established around Europe in the 1990s, aimed at hosting technology companies (the German *Neuer Markt*, the French *Nouveau Marchè* and the Italian *Nuovo Mercato* among others) and representing the European answer to the Nasdaq. The experience had only limited success; the burst of the dot-com bubble in 2001 pushed the capitalization to record lows while insider trading scandals and accounting frauds tarnished their reputation.

Bonardo *et al.* (2011) analyze a panel of 499 high-tech companies that went public in Europe between 1995 and 2003; they show that the affiliation with a university enhances valuation, in particular when academics are present in the top management team. However, in the long run, university-based companies exhibit worse operating performance than other technology firms. Similar results are obtained in a study by Colombo *et al.* (2019) focusing on biotech companies.

Bessler and Bittelmeyer (2008) study the patenting activity by companies that went public on the German Neuer Markt; they claim that patents are a reliable indicator for the performance of start-up technology firms that went public and that the valuation effects are more pronounced for higher quality patents. Similarly, Useche (2014) finds that patents can be signals of the IPO company quality and are associated with larger amounts of money raised.

The second group of reasons for going public has positive indirect effects on the company. In particular, access to the stock market means a parallel reduction in the cost of debt: this may be due to the greater bargaining power of the listed company in negotiating contracts thanks to an improvement in its reputation on the one hand, and on the other hand it could be related to the decrease in its leverage, which in turn reduces the perceived risk associated with it (Pagano *et al.*, 1998). In general, being subject to market scrutiny reduces asymmetric information and the cost of finding information about the company for other stakeholders. In turn, this can improve the diversification of financial sources. Increased visibility and the upgrading of the company image to the status of being a listed company also translates into benefits of a managerial nature. Indeed, the obligation to issue information before and after the listing contributes to both increasing the company's credibility and improving its standing with potential suppliers, clients, and industrial partners (Stoughton and Zechner, 1998). This can lead to greater bargaining power in negotiating contracts with suppliers and clients, as well as creating opportunities to form partnerships with competitors or counterparts in the same business.

Moreover, the IPO can become a particularly important marketing tool for innovative companies in terms of developing customer loyalty and knowledge of the market (Demers and Lewellen, 2003; Maksimovic and Pichler, 2001). Other indirect benefits arise out of the company shares being listed on a regulated market. For example, Holmström and Tirole (1993) argue that a listed company can benefit from carrying out plans for share-based returns. These plans aim to motivate and develop loyalty in the company management and "key" figures. This is, even more, the case with young and innovative companies, often characterized by the importance of human resources to the company (Rocholl, 2005).

In the third group of decisive factors the decision to go public is not only for the company's benefit but fundamentally also positively impacts on the existing shareholders. The IPO offering improves liquidity (the literature defines marketability as the premium on the share price involved in the company transition from private to public) and the opportunity for the founders-shareholders to diversify their portfolio and to monetize part of the investment in the company (Mello and Parsons, 1998). In some cases, the offering can also ease the "generational transition".

Table 2.1: Benefits and costs of going public

Benefits of IPO	Costs of IPO
• Access finance to fund company growth	• Costs of commissions for the offering
• Balancing of company financial structure and reduced exposure to risk	• Informational costs required to obtain and maintain the status of listed company
• Improved bargaining power in negotiating contracts	• Enlargement of share ownership
• Company's reputation improves	• Loss of autonomy in the decision making
• Facilitates external expansion through acquisitions	• Problems created by greater company disclosure
• Opportunity for the existing shareholders to cash in	• Problems from reduction in the benefits of being private
• Opportunity to solve the problem of the generational transition	

Besides generating business advantages for the company, the IPO process can introduce a series of additional costs and constraints. In particular, some of these are the direct result of the listing, i.e., the commission for the offering and the cost of providing information, while other costs are incurred indirectly, such as for organizational and management restructuring. Indeed, an IPO also has "non-monetary" consequences: widening the share ownership impedes the speed of decision making and needs a more bureaucratic organizational structure. Secondly, the informational transparency required, while on the one hand being seen as a means of communicating with the market, is often perceived as a requirement that both imposes additional costs and creates problems with disclosure. Table 2.1 summarizes the main advantages and disadvantages of IPOs recognized in the economic-financial literature.

Several temporal modeling studies of the decision to go public have recently been published. They identify the circumstances in which the benefits for liquidity and for diversification provided by floating on the stock market are greater than the "benefits of being private" enjoyed by an unlisted company. The limit identified in the previous literature is that going public is a one-shot decision. To this extent, the new models study the decision to go public from a temporal perspective taking into account the option to "re-privatize" the company in the future. An example is put forward by Benninga and Helmantel (2005) who develop an IPO timing model comparing gains of diversification against the benefits of being private. Continuing on the theme of the time-line between public and private ownership, two other articles presented by Boot *et al.* (2006) and by Rocholl (2005) are worth mentioning. These take the point of view of corporate governance and compare the limits imposed by going public in terms of how rigid governance becomes and the degree to which the company's decision making is autonomous, with a lower cost of capital being associated with improved liquidity. The structure of governance and the opportunity for shareholders to diversify their portfolio pre-IPO is also the basis of a study by Bodnaruk *et al.* (2008) who demonstrate how companies with less diversified shareholders have a greater probability of going public. Refer to Audretsch and Lehmann (2014) for a review of corporate governance mechanisms, and specifically to Lehmann and Vismara (2020) for corporate governance of IPOs.

Lastly, by interviewing 300 American Chief Financial Officers (CFOs), Brau and Fawcett (2006) compare theory with practice. The main reason for an IPO is found to be the creation of liquidity and the need to define a price for the shares in the company to facilitate acquisition processes, either cash- or stock-financed (Zingales, 1995). On the other hand, CFOs give less credit to reasons connected with the cost of capital and the financial structure. Celikyurt *et al.* (2010) show that IPO firms' M&A activity outpaces that of mature firms in the same industries. According to Hovakimian and Hutton (2010) and Hsieh *et al.* (2011) going public dramatically reduces uncertainty about the bidder company's value and allows to better estimate the value added by the acquisition.

The motivations driving firms to conduct an IPO or to engage in M&As are numerous and well analyzed by scholars. Financial literature helps to highlight the most influential ones. Until the beginning of the 1980s, the decision to go public was simply considered as a growth stage: companies reach a certain point in life in which entrepreneurial capital (or debt) is no longer able to sustain the survival or the expansion of the business. Raising funds by selling stock to the public is a solution. However, this interpretation can no longer be the main reason for taking companies public. Starting with Pagano (1993), the IPO decision has been modeled as a trade-off between the costs and the benefits associated. On the cost side, the two major losses for issuers are underpricing and registration and advisory expenses. Together, they can reach 30% of the capital raised (Ritter, 1987). Other less quantifiable costs are associated with agency issues arising from the separation of ownership and control (Jensen and Meckling, 1976). Moreover, public companies are required to guarantee a certain degree of transparency by providing periodical disclosure. Conversely, increased visibility for the company, higher liquidity, the possibility to rebalance the firm's capital structure, lower cost of debt and diversification are the main benefits. Corporate control motivations are also crucial: IPOs offer a way to shareholders to reduce their stake in the company or to regain control by allowing venture capitalists to cash out. Anderson *et al.* (2017) demonstrate that some characteristics of the IPO company and process predict M&A activity. These characteristics include underwriter quality, promotional activity, pricing, proceeds, ownership structure, and issuance activity suggestive of market timing. Investors appear to rely on these observable aspects of a firm's going public process to anticipate the implications of M&A activity for security valuation.

The M&A activity has an impact on the follow-up performance of IPO firms. Brau *et al.* (2012) highlight that acquirers exhibit a significant negative underperformance compared to non-acquirers. Arikan and Stulz (2016) establish that, while younger IPO firms make more related and diversifying acquisitions than mature firms, the acquisition rate follows a U-shape over firms' life cycle after the listing. Consistent with neoclassical theories, acquiring firms have better performance and growth opportunities and create wealth through acquisitions of nonpublic firms throughout their life. Consistent with agency theories, older firms experience negative stock price reactions for acquisitions of public firms.

IPO firms may engage in acquisitions, but are also more easily to be acquired through a takeover on the market. Field and Karpoff (2002) show that newly listed companies are more likely to deploy takeover defenses when managers' compensation is high, shareholdings are small, and oversight from nonmanagerial shareholders is weak. Meoli *et al.* (2013) study 254 biotech firms that went public in Europe between 1990 and 2009; they find that affiliation with a university enhances the probability of being targeted in subsequent M&As, particularly in cross-border deals. They conclude that after the IPO, acquisitions by incumbent firms are mechanisms to finalize the technology transfer process started in a research institute.

Signori and Vismara (2017) document that 16.3% of the population of 3,433 firms going public in Europe from 1995 to 2009 became acquirers within three years of the IPO, while 16.8% are targeted. Firms with more liquid stocks are more likely to acquire and complete a larger number of stock-financed acquisitions. More liquid firms are also more likely to be acquired, and at higher valuations. The results suggest that firms should time their IPO based on liquidity considerations to facilitate subsequent M&A activity as either acquirer or target.

Ragozzino and Reuer (2011) focus the attention on the geographical dimension of acquisitions of IPO firms. They find that some signals (i.e., financial backing from VCs, the reputation of the lead underwriter and the initial underpricing) are important to reduce information asymmetry and facilitate cross-border acquisitions. Signori and Vismara (2018) document that cycles in IPO activity can be explained by the small firms' increasing preference for being acquired rather than growing independently.

A recent trend in the market for IPOs has been the flow of SPACs (special purpose acquisition vehicles). Those are shell companies, that raise money on the market and are intended to combine with a privately-owned company through a reverse merger.

Kolb and Tykvová (2016) discuss how private firms tend to use SPACs as an alternative way to get listed, particularly in years with weak IPO activity and volatile markets. In 2008 and 2009, approximately 31% of firms went public through a SPAC acquisition rather than through an IPO. Companies going public by business combination with

SPACs are more likely to be small and levered firms with low growth opportunities. The authors also find that SPAC firms are associated with severe underperformance in comparison to the market, the industry and comparable IPO firms.

Table 2.2 presents a summary of some of the most significant studies on the decision to go public. More recently, the literature has compared the decision to go public through initial public offerings on traditional stock markets with alternatives, such equity crowdfunding offerings (Farag and Johan, 2021): we believe that this is a promising research stream for the future. One of such examples comes from the study of information cascades (Bikhchandani *et al.*, 1992, 1998; Welch, 1992). In IPOs, late investors alter their own valuations by observing the behavior of previous investors (Aggarwal *et al.*, 2002; Amihud *et al.*, 2003). IPOs with high levels of institutional demand in the early days of bookbuilding also see high levels of bids from retail investors in the later days (Khurshed *et al.*, 2014). This explains why IPOs typically result in either over-subscription or under-subscription, with very few cases in between. In IPOs, however, the information available to the public about the nature of the bids is limited to the distinction between institutional and retail investors. Equity crowdfunding platforms, instead, reveal online the (nick)name of the investor for each bid. This availability of information at an individual level is unique and offers a privileged avenue to investigate information cascades among individual investors. Vismara (2018) shows that information cascades among individual investors are crucial for the success of crowdfunding campaigns. In particular, public profile investors increase the appeal of the offer already among early investors, who in turn mediate the effect of public profile investors on the success of the offerings.

Table 2.2: Literature on the cost of going public

Authors	Journal	Key Findings
Abrahamson *et al.* (2011)	Journal of Finance	The increasing incidence of 7% fee for larger issues in US IPOs is consistent with strategic pricing and in line with models of implicit collusion, even considering the entry by European investment banks and a fall-off in the number of IPOs.
Acharya and Xu (2017)	Journal of Financial Economics	In this paper, they examine the relation between innovation and a firm's financial dependence using a sample of privately held and publicly traded US firms. They find that public firms in external finance dependent industries spend more on research and development and generate a better patent portfolio than their private counterparts. However, public firms in internal finance dependent industries do not have a better innovation profile than private firms. The results are robust to various empirical strategies that address selection bias. The findings indicate that the influence of public listing on innovation depends on the need for external capital.
Aslan and Kumar (2011)	Journal of Financial and Quantitative Analysis	Is the decision to go public or private a stock-market-driven "sideshow" or does it have significant effects on investment and profitability? The authors address this issue using a comprehensive data set of private and public companies in the UK during 1996–2006. Firms with high investment-financing needs, lower information-production costs, and high industry market-to-book ratios are more likely to go public. In contrast to the literature, they find that capital investment and profitability increase substantially after the initial public offering (IPO). Consistent with the agency-cost-based theories of going private, firms decrease investment but increase profits after going private, especially firms bought out by private equity investors. Our analysis also highlights the effects of market conditions on the ownership structure decision.

Continued.

Table 2.2: Continued

Authors	Journal	Key Findings
Bernstein (2015)	Journal of Finance	This paper investigates the effects of going public on innovation by comparing the innovation activity of firms that go public with firms that withdraw their initial public offering (IPO) filing and remain private. NASDAQ fluctuations during the bookbuilding phase are used as an instrument for IPO completion. Using patent-based metrics, the author finds that the quality of internal innovation declines following the IPO, and firms experience both an exodus of skilled inventors and a decline in the productivity of the remaining inventors. However, public firms attract new human capital and acquire external innovation. The analysis reveals that going public changes firms' strategies in pursuing innovation.
Bessembinder *et al.* (2015)	Journal of Finance	The authors examine the effects of secondary market liquidity on firm value and the IPO decision. Competitive aftermarket liquidity provision is associated with reduced welfare and a discounted secondary market price that can dissuade IPOs. The competitive market fails in particular for firms or at times when uncertainty regarding fundamental value and asymmetric information are large in combination. In these cases, firm value and welfare are improved by a contract where the firm engages a designated market maker to enhance liquidity. Such contracts represent a market solution to a market imperfection, particularly for small, growth firms.

Continued.

Table 2.2: Continued

Authors	Journal	Key Findings
Billings and Lewis-Western (2016)	Contemporary Accounting Research	Prior research suggests that the fear of litigation precludes most managers from manipulating earnings in the initial public offering (IPO) setting. Yet, managers' restraint is perhaps unwarranted: research has not yet linked instances of aggressive pre-IPO reporting to increased litigation risk. This paper investigates when aggressive IPO reporting triggers legal consequences. Examining 2,037 IPOs, the authors find that even when ex post evidence indicates the presence of earnings inflation, litigation is more likely to occur when investors have relied on the suspect earnings during the pricing process. Why might investors rely on some firms' abnormal accruals when valuing the IPO and yet discount the abnormal accruals of other firms? The analyses suggest that IPO investors incorporate abnormal accrual information into IPO prices in situations where sources of information are lacking or are less reliable. In these situations, they find that abnormal accruals do positively correlate with future performance, validating investors' use of this information when pricing these offerings. Yet, when ex post performance reveals that these pre-IPO abnormal accruals were in fact inflated, they find that litigation emerges to allow harmed shareholders to recover losses incurred dating back to the pricing process—importantly, investors are only harmed if they used those abnormal accruals in pricing the IPO. Collectively, their evidence indicates that litigation in response to earnings inflation does indeed surface in the IPO setting—but only when investors need it to settle the score.
Bustamante (2012)	Review of Finance	This paper develops a real options model in which firms may use the timing of their initial public offerings (IPO) to signal the quality of their investment prospects to outside investors. When adverse selection is more relevant (cold markets), firms with better investment prospects accelerate their IPO relative to their perfect information benchmark to reveal their type to outside investors. When adverse selection is less relevant (hot markets), all firms issue simultaneously, issuers are younger on average, and IPO timing is uninformative. An extension with multiple signals and the empirical evidence show that better ranked firms are younger, issue a lower fraction of shares, and underprice more during cold markets, and that issuers are younger on average during hot markets.

Continued.

Table 2.2: Continued

Authors	Journal	Key Findings
Chaplinsky *et al.* (2017)	Journal of Accounting Research	The authors of this paper examine the effects of Title I of the Jumpstart Our Business Startups Act for a sample of 312 emerging growth companies (EGCs) that filed for an initial public offering (IPO) from April 5, 2012 through April 30, 2015. They find no reduction in the direct costs of issuance, accounting, legal, or underwriting fees for EGC IPOs. Underpricing, an indirect cost of issuance that increases an issuer's cost of capital, is significantly higher for EGCs compared to other IPOs. More importantly, greater underpricing is present only for larger firms that are newly eligible for scaled disclosure under the Act. Overall, they find little evidence that the Act in its first three years has reduced the measurable costs of going public. Although there are benefits of the Act that issuers appear to value, they should be balanced against the higher costs of capital that can occur after its enactment.
Chemmanur and He (2011)	Journal of Financial Economics	The authors develop a new rationale for initial public offering (IPO) waves based on product market considerations. Two firms, with differing productivity levels, compete in an industry with a significant probability of a positive productivity shock. Going public, though costly, not only allows a firm to raise external capital cheaply, but also enables it to grab market share from its private competitors. They solve for the decision of each firm to go public versus remain private, and the optimal timing of going public. In equilibrium, even firms with sufficient internal capital to fund their new investment may go public, driven by the possibility of their product market competitors going public. IPO waves may arise in equilibrium even in industries which do not experience a productivity shock. Their model predicts that firms going public during an IPO wave will have lower productivity and post-IPO profitability but larger cash holdings than those going public off the wave; it makes similar predictions for firms going public later versus earlier in an IPO wave. They empirically test and find support for these predictions.
Dalziel *et al.* (2011)	Journal of Management Studies	The initial public offering (IPO) of a new venture's stock often results in significant changes to the firm's ownership structure. Because firm owners (principals) often have heterogeneous interests, conflicts can arise among the principals. While governance mechanisms are often effective in limiting agency problems, the authors suggest that principals can also attempt to use governance mechanisms to their own advantage at IPO settings. Specifically, when principal–principal conflict exists, powerful principals may exert control via governance mechanisms to pursue their own interests in ways that create inefficiencies in the form of "principal costs".

Continued.

Table 2.2: Continued

Authors	Journal	Key Findings
Dambra *et al.* (2015)	Journal of Financial Economics	In April 2012, the Jumpstart Our Business Startups Act (JOBSAct) was enacted to help revitalize the initial public offering (IPO) market, especially for small firms. During the year ending March 2014, IP volume and the proportion of small firm issuers was the largest since 2000. Controlling for market conditions, the authors estimate that the JOBS Act has led to 21 additional IPOs annually, a 25% increase over pre-JOBS levels. Firms with high proprietary disclosure costs, such as biotechnology and pharmaceutical firms, increase IPO activity the most. These firms are also more likely to take advantage of the act's de-risking provisions, allowing firms to file the IPO confidentially while testing-the-waters.
Hsieh *et al.* (2011)	Journal of Financial and Quantitative Analysis	The authors propose a model that links a firm's decision to go public with its subsequent takeover strategy. A private bidder does not know a firm's true valuation, which affects its gain from a potential takeover. Consequently, a private bidder pursues a suboptimal restructuring policy. An alternative route is to complete an initial public offering (IPO) first. An IPO reduces valuation uncertainty, leading to a more efficient acquisition strategy, therefore enhancing firm value. They calibrate the model using data on IPOs and mergers and acquisitions (M&As). The resulting comparative statics generate several novel qualitative and quantitative predictions, which complement the predictions of other theories linking IPOs and M&As. For example, the time it takes a newly public firm to attempt an acquisition of another firm is expected to increase in the degree of valuation uncertainty prior to the firm's IPO and in the cost of going public, and it is expected to decrease in the valuation surprise realized at the time of the IPO. They find strong empirical support for the model's predictions.
Hsu *et al.* (2010)	Journal of Finance	The authors analyze the effect of initial public offerings (IPOs) on industry competitors and provide evidence that companies experience negative stock price reactions to completed IPOs in their industry and positive stock price reactions to their withdrawal. Following a successful IPO in their industry, they show significant deterioration in their operating performance. These results are consistent with the existence of IPO related competitive advantages through the loosening of financial constraints, financial intermediary certification, and the presence of knowledge capital. These aspects of competitiveness are significant in explaining the cross-section of underperformance as well as survival probabilities for competing firms.

Continued.

Table 2.2: Continued

Authors	Journal	Key Findings
Lee *et al.* (2011)	Strategic Entrepreneurship Journal	Would an initial public offering (IPO) in a growing and uncertain industry have a positive or negative effect on directly competing incumbent firms in the industry? The authors of this paper assert that due to the risk and uncertainty inherent in a growing industry, a firm's IPO may send a positive market signal of growing industry demand. An IPO can send a signal to the investors of directly competing incumbents that the market is promising, and incumbent firms will enjoy a better future. If directly competing incumbent firms are capable of capturing these positive externalities, they will experience even greater positive results. In particular, an incumbent firm with a significant research and development investment may capture more of this increased demand in the industry. On the other hand, if a market segment is more concentrated, it is more likely that directly competing incumbents will suffer when another firm announces an IPO. They find supporting results for the various arguments of our initial question examining the computer related service industry. They also present discussion and implications for the results.
Leittertorf and Rau (2014)	Strategic Management Journal	Socioemotional wealth (SEW), i.e., the noneconomic utility a family derives from its ownership position in a firm, is the primary reference point for family firms. Family firms are willing to sacrifice economic gains in order to preserve their noneconomic utility. Thus, the authors argue that family firms sacrifice IPO proceeds by choosing higher IPO underpricing than nonfamily firms if underpricing helps them protect their SEW. Their empirical results, based on a sample of 153 German IPOs, support the hypothesis. On average, family firms have 10 percentage points more IPO underpricing than nonfamily firms.
Liu *et al.* (2014a)	Strategic Management Journal	This paper examines the diffusion of information around the initial public offering (IPO) process and identifies transaction partners on which IPO firms are dependent. Using a resource payments perspective, the authors argue that this dependence will lead to greater cumulative abnormal stock returns for transaction partners when this information is revealed in the market (when the initial form S-1 is filed with the SEC). Moreover, they examine the uniqueness of the resource configuration between the IPO firm and transaction partners and find that greater uniqueness is associated with higher valuation for these transaction partners. They also find that multiple dependencies (by the IPO firm) reduce the valuation effect for transaction partners, indicating that a bargaining effect reduces the potential value that any transaction partner can appropriate.

Continued.

Table 2.2: Continued

Authors	Journal	Key Findings
Ragozzino and Reuer (2011)	Strategic Management Journal	This paper examines acquisitions of firms after they have undergone IPOs. Combining insights from information economics with recent research on geographic distance in various market settings, the analysis investigates whether the presence or absence of different signals on IPO firms has an impact on the geographic proximity of acquirers. The central proposition the authors develop and test is that specific characteristics of IPOs—venture capitalist backing, investment bank reputation, and underpricing of issued shares—convey signals on these firms, which can facilitate acquisitions by more remote acquirers who are more likely to face the risk of adverse selection.
Wu (2012)	Organization Science	This paper investigates whether and how going public affects firm innovation. The author proposes that initial public offerings (IPOs) fundamentally reshape core organizational structures and processes, this creating implications for firms' overall innovative productivity and their exploratory search strategies. Using longitudinal data on US medical device firms funded by venture capital and inverse probability of treatment weights to account for self-selection into IPOs and the presence of time-dependent confounders, she finds that a firm's overall innovative productivity increases after the firm goes public. Going public also decreases the proportion of innovation search that explores new and recently developed knowledge and increases the proportion of exploratory search building on scientific knowledge. Estimates represent population average treatment effects.

3

Pricing and Valuation

Valuing IPOs is a challenging task given the nature of the issuers, that are often young companies with limited track records, for which it is difficult to forecast future growth prospects. In addition, underwriters are subject to a conflict of interest when valuing IPOs, since they simultaneously have to deal with issuers and investors, whose objective functions are often conflicting (Baron, 1982). While issuers tend to be more focused on the maximization of offering proceeds, investors tend to be more satisfied in presence of "hot" (i.e., underpriced) IPO allocations. The objective of this section is to provide a picture of how the IPO valuation process is carried out by underwriters, in terms of which methodologies are used and how they are implemented. While disclosure of the valuation methods used by IPO underwriters to estimate the offer price is very limited in the United States, more information is available in Continental Europe, which makes it an ideal setting where to pursue the objective of this study.

There are different methods to value a firm. Asset-based valuation models rely on the estimation of the fair market value of an IPO company's single assets and the equity value is computed after deducting other liabilities. The asset-based method disregards a company's

25

prospective opportunities and growth; therefore, it is most appropriate for companies with stable profits and a high proportion of current assets and current liabilities and few/insignificant intangible assets. Discounted cash flow (DCF) models rely on the estimation of future free cash flows generated by the IPO company, for all investors (free cash flows to the firm, asset-side) or shareholders only (free cash flow to equity, equity-side). Cash flows, including eventually a terminal value of the business, are then discounted to compute the present value with an appropriate cost of capital. DCF models are well suited to estimate growth companies, startups and in general unprofitable companies that are expected to become profitable in the future.

Relative valuation is a simple methodology, according to which the value of an IPO company is compared to the values assessed by the market for comparable listed companies in the same business. Price multiples referring either to the current earnings, equity book value, revenues or other business-specific accounting variables are computed and then applied to the IPO company, controlling for the differences between the firms that might affect the multiple. Relative valuation is based on the assumption that companies in the same business share the same market opportunities and threats and have similar cost functions and productivity, so they should be evaluated homogenously. Relative valuation is commonly adopted in IPO pricing and the process is typically disclosed in the IPO prospectus.

When the IPO company valuation exceeds $1 billion, the firm is labeled as a "unicorn". Market data show a significant increase in the number of "unicorn" IPOs in the last five years (Gornall and Strebulaev, 2020), with public markets valuing high-growth companies at better multiples compared to private transactions (source: Crunchbase). This is a topic that could be investigated by scholars in the next years.

Bookbuilding, as described in the next section, is the most diffused process to decide on the final IPO price in the world (Sherman, 2005). Typically, an initial price range using the valuation techniques described above is determined and published in the official prospectus. The final offer price is set according to private and public information collected during the offering.

A few studies have investigated the pricing mechanisms in IPOs. First, Kim and Ritter (1999) examine the use of multiples of comparable companies to value IPOs. They consider both historical accounting figures and forecasted earnings; they find that price-to-earnings (P/E) ratios dominate all other multiples in terms of valuation accuracy. Purnanandam and Swaminathan (2004) study the US IPO market and find that the median listing company is overvalued by about 50% with respect to its industry comparables. Their results have been criticized by Zheng (2007): he considers the dilution effects of newly issued shares and adjusts for cash holdings and leverage when calculating the IPO firm price multiples so that they are consistent with the accounting variables. He also controls for expected growth when selecting matching firms. After these adjustments, he finds that the IPO firms are not significantly overvalued. The same conclusion is shared by Houston et al. (2006); they study the target prices established by analysts one month after the IPO and argue that this indicates how US investment bankers value IPOs. They infer that offer prices are set at a discount of 10% compared to the mean comparable firm multiple used to set the target price one month later. However, this discount is not significantly different from zero.

The study by Kim and Ritter compares the valuation of companies going public with one of the peers selected using alternative procedures (e.g., industry matching), but has no information on how the offer price is set. Conversely, a number of studies on European IPOs shed some light on the valuation techniques implemented by underwriters, with evidence from the Italian (Cassia et al., 2004), the French (Roosenboom, 2007, 2012) and the Belgian (Deloof et al., 2009) markets.

First, Cassia et al. (2004) investigate how the peer comparable approach has been used for the valuation of companies that went public on the Italian *Nuovo Mercato*. In Italy, IPO prospectuses often report the valuation methods used by investment banks. This allowed analyzing for the first time the accuracy of "real-world" valuation estimates. The paper shows that underwriters rely on price-to-book and price-earnings multiples. The valuation estimates generated by these multiples are closest to offer prices. Conversely, when using enterprise value ratios comparable firms' multiples are typically higher than those of the firms going public. The study concludes that underwriters can select comparables that make their valuations look conservative. About specific multiples, both Cassia *et al.* (2004) and Deloof *et al.* (2009) document that price-to-earnings (P/E) and price-to-cash flow (P/CF) ratios are the preferred valuation multiples in Italy and Belgium. Deloof *et al.* (2009) investigate IPO valuation by investment banks for 49 IPOs on Euronext Brussels in the 1993–2001 period. They find that for each IPO several valuation methods are used, of which the DCF is the most popular. Their results suggest that the discounting expected dividends tends to underestimate value.

Roosenboom (2007) investigates how French underwriters value the stocks of IPO companies and find that several alternative valuation methods are adopted: peer group multiples valuation, the dividend discount model, the discounted cash flow model, the residual income method (which is a variant of the DCF method), and underwriter-specific methods. Underwriters choose a particular valuation method considering firm characteristics, aggregate stock market returns, and aggregate stock market volatility in the period before the IPO. In addition, underwriters combine the value estimates of the valuation methods they use into a fair value by assigning weights to these value estimates. Interestingly, valuations are more conservative for companies that are brought to the market by less reputable underwriters and that are forecasted to be less profitable. Roosenboom (2012) argues that underwriters deliberately discount the fair value estimate when setting the preliminary offer price; they advertise this price discount in an attempt to augment investor participation in the placement. This results in higher price updates of the preliminary offer price that partially recover the discount.

The selection of the set of peer listed companies is relevant in the pricing of IPO shares and to some extent arbitrary: underwriters may be tempted to choose comparable companies that make the offer price look conservative. The correct selection of the peer group requires the solution of a trade-off between more of less strict selection criteria: if they are too strict, few or no comparable companies will be identified; if they are generic, the risk is to obtain a biased valuation.

Interestingly, Paleari *et al.* (2014) find that underwriters systematically exclude candidate comparable firms that make a given IPO appear overvalued. On average, comparable firms published in official prospectuses have 13%–38% higher valuation multiples than those obtained from matching algorithms or selected by sell-side analysts, including the same underwriter's analyst after the IPO. Even if IPOs are priced at a discount as compared to peers selected by the underwriters, they are still at a premium with regard to alternatively selected peers.

Vismara *et al.* (2015) compare the selection of peer firms made by investment banks as underwriters at the IPO with that done shortly thereafter as analysts. They find that several times there is a change in the composition of the group. The peers published in the IPO prospectuses have higher valuations than those published in the post-IPO equity research reports of the same firm, especially if the underwriter is US-based. The authors argue that underwriters select comparable firms that make IPO shares look conservatively priced, while this conflict of interest tends to fade afterward. The upward bias in peer selection is larger for underwriters with greater market power and lower for regular players in the IPO market.

Kaplan and Ruback (1995) compare the performance of the discounted cash flow estimates to that of estimates obtained from the peer approach, relying on companies in similar industries and involved in similar transactions. The discounted cash flow methods are found to perform at least as well as the comparable methods. However, the authors rely on a very limited sample, because DCF estimates from the underwriters are rarely publicly available. The same conclusion emerges from the study by Berkman *et al.* (2000) who consider the IPO market in New Zealand.

Aggarwal *et al.* (2009) examine how IPO valuation has changed over time from 1986 to 2001 and find that firms with more negative earnings have higher valuations than do firms with less negative earnings and firms with more positive earnings have higher valuations than firms with less positive earnings. The results suggest that negative earnings are a proxy for growth opportunities and that such growth options are a significant component of IPO firm value.

Cogliati *et al.* (2011) and Bonaventura and Giudici (2017) develop a set of "reverse engineering" models to discover the short term profitability implied in the IPO prices. They show that there is a significant optimistic bias in the estimation of future profitability compared to ex-post actual realization and that the forecast error is larger the faster has been the recent growth of the company, the higher is the leverage of the IPO firm, the more companies issued equity on the market.

Specific IPO firm characteristics are found to be incorporated by the market when pricing IPO shares: the quality of the entrepreneurial team (Chemmanur *et al.*, 2020), the presence of domestic or foreign venture capitalists in the shareholding (Chahine *et al.*, 2019), the affiliation with prestigious underwriters (Khoury *et al.*, 2013), the strategies of technology commercialization (Morricone *et al.*, 2017), the visibility on social networks (Mumi *et al.*, 2019). Refer to Manigart and Wright (2013) for a review of research on VCs.

The literature also highlights that the IPO valuation process may be biased by the issuing company through earnings management practices. Friedlan (1994) shows that issuers make income-increasing discretionary accruals in the financial statements released before the offering to attract the interest of intermediaries and potential investors. Yet, according to Nagata and Hachiya (2007) underwriters discount such misconduct and adjust their valuation accordingly.

Table 3.1 presents a summary of some of the most important studies on the valuation of IPOs.

Table 3.1: Literature on IPO pricing and valuation

Authors	Journal	Key Findings
Aggarwal et al. (2009)	Financial Management	The work examines how IPO valuation has changed over time by focusing on three time periods: 1986–1990, January 1997 to March 2000 (designated as a "hot issue" period), and April 2000 to December 2001 (the burst of the dot-com bubble). Using a sample of 1,655 IPOs, the authors find that firms with more negative earnings have higher valuations than do firms with less negative earnings and firms with more positive earnings have higher valuations than firms with less positive earnings.
Berkman et al. (2000)	Journal of International Financial Management and Accounting	The authors compare estimates of IPO share value derived from conventional discounted cash flow and price earnings valuation methods to the market price. For a sample of 45 firms newly listed on the New Zealand Stock Exchange the results suggest that the discounted cash flow method and the peer approach have similar accuracy.
Bonaventura and Giudici (2017)	Eurasian Business Review	The valuation process of companies listed on the Italian Exchange in the period 2000–2009 at the IPO is considered. Through a "reverse engineering" model the short term profitability implied in the offer prices is computed. A significant optimistic bias in the estimation of future profitability compared to ex-post actual realization is found and the mean forecast error is substantially large. The forecast error is larger the faster has been the recent growth of the company, the higher is the leverage of the IPO firm, the more companies issued equity on the market in the same time window.
Cogliati et al. (2011)	Annals of Finance	The paper studies the valuation of companies going public and defines a methodology to infer the growth expectations implicit in the prices of the IPO. Applying the procedure to a sample of IPOs in three European countries (France, Italy, and Germany), the cash flow growth implied by offer prices and the bias of implied growth in comparison to the realized are computed. The estimated growth in cash flow is much higher than its actual realization, with the median IPO firm overvalued at the offering by 74%. Estimation errors increase with IPO firms' leverage and underpricing, and decrease with age, size, and book-to-market ratios.

Continued.

Table 3.1: Continued

Authors	Journal	Key Findings
Deloof *et al.* (2009)	Journal of Business Finance and Accounting	The authors analyze the valuation and the pricing of 49 Belgian IPOs in the 1993–2001 period. They find that for each IPO several valuation methods are used, of which Discounted Free Cash Flow (DFCF) is the most popular. The offer price is mainly based on DFCF valuation, to which a discount is applied. When using multiples, investment banks rely mostly on future earnings and cash flows. Multiples based on post-IPO forecasted earnings and cash flows result in more accurate valuations.
Friedlan (1994)	Contemporary Accounting Research	The author reports evidence that IPO issuers make income-increasing discretionary accruals in the financial statements released before the offering. This evidence is consistent with the hypothesis that issuers believe that financial statement information affects IPO offering prices.
Houston *et al.* (2006)	Journal of Financial and Quantitative Analysis	The work considers how analysts establish target prices for IPO firms and whether comparable firms used to support target prices are helpful in explaining IPO offer prices. During the bubble period of 1999 to 2000, the average offer price was set at a discount relative to comparable firm valuations. In contrast, the average offer price was set at a small premium relative to comparables in the pre-bubble period. The shift appears to hold even after controlling for the differences in the types of firms going public during the bubble period. A possible explanation is that the shift arose because underwriters and analysts faced different incentives and legal exposures during the bubble period.
Kaplan and Ruback (1995)	Journal of Finance	The article compares the market value of highly leveraged transactions (HLTs) to the discounted value of their corresponding cash flow forecasts. For a sample of 51 HLTs completed between 1983 and 1989, the valuations of discounted cash flow forecasts are within 10%, on average, of the market values of the completed transactions. The valuations perform at least as well as valuation methods using comparable companies and transactions.

Continued.

Table 3.1: Continued

Authors	Journal	Key Findings
Kim and Ritter (1999)	Journal of Financial Economics	The authors explore the use of accounting information in conjunction with comparable firm multiples in valuing IPOs. They find that the price-earnings (P/E), market-to-book, and price-to-sales multiples of comparable firms have only modest predictive ability without further adjustments. This is largely due to the wide variation of these ratios for young firms within an industry. P/E multiples using forecasted earnings result in much more accurate valuations than multiples using trailing earnings.
Nagata and Hachiya (2007)	Review of Pacific Basin Financial Markets and Policies	The study investigates whether the extent of earnings management has any impact on offer price in IPOs. Using a sample of 581 JASDAQ IPO firms, the authors find that firms with conservative earnings management tend to have higher offer prices, and firms managing earnings aggressively tend to be discounted when they fail to exhibit smooth earnings growth. The results are consistent with the hypothesis that underwriters adjust for the effect of earnings management to appropriately price the issues.
Paleari et al. (2014)	Financial Management	The authors argue that valuing IPOs using multiples allows underwriters discretion when selecting comparable firms. They systematically exclude candidate comparable firms that make a given IPO appear overvalued. On average, comparable firms published in official prospectuses have higher valuation multiples than those obtained from matching algorithms or selected by sell-side analysts, including the same underwriter's analyst after the IPO. Even if IPOs are priced at a discount as compared to peers selected by the underwriters, they are still at a premium with regard to alternatively selected peers.
Purnanandam and Swaminathan (2004)	The Review of Financial Studies	The work finds that in a sample of more than 2,000 IPOs from 1980 to 1997, the median IPO was significantly overvalued at the offer price relative to valuations based on industry peer price multiples. This overvaluation ranges from 14% to 50% depending on the peer matching criteria. Cross-sectional regressions show that "overvalued" IPOs provide high first-day returns, but low long-run risk-adjusted returns. These overvalued IPOs have lower profitability, higher accruals, and higher analyst growth forecasts than "undervalued" IPOs. Ex post, the projected high growth of overvalued IPOs fails to materialize, while their profitability declines from pre-IPO levels. These results suggest that IPO investors are deceived by optimistic growth forecasts and pay insufficient attention to profitability in valuing IPO.

Continued.

Table 3.1: Continued

Authors	Journal	Key Findings
Roosenboom (2007)	Contemporary Accounting Research	The paper investigates the methods adopted by French underwriters to value the stocks of IPO companies: peer group multiples valuation, the dividend discount model, the discounted cash flow model, the economic value-added method, and underwriter-specific methods. The choice is driven by firm characteristics, aggregate stock market returns, and aggregate stock market volatility in the period before the IPO.
Roosenboom (2012)	Journal of Banking and Finance	The paper documents that underwriters employ multiples valuation, dividend discount models and discounted cash flow (DCF) analysis to determine the IPO fair value but all of these valuation methods suffer from a positive bias with respect to equilibrium market value. Underwriters deliberately discount the fair value estimate when setting the preliminary offer price. Part of the intentional price discount can be recovered by higher price updates. Controlling for other factors such as investor demand, part of underpricing stems from this intentional price discount.
Vismara *et al.* (2015)	Journal of Corporate Finance	The authors compare the selection of peer firms made by investment banks as underwriters at the IPO with that done shortly thereafter as analysts. Three out of seven comparable firms, on average, are changed. The peers published in the IPO prospectuses have higher valuations than those published in the post-IPO equity research reports of the same firm, especially if the underwriter is US-based. It is argued that underwriters select comparable firms that make the issuer's shares look conservatively priced at the IPO, while this conflict of interest tends to fade afterwards. The upward bias in peer selection is larger for underwriters with greater market power, and lower for repeat players in the IPO market.
Zheng (2007)	Journal of Empirical Finance	While generally the literature posits that IPOs are overvalued at the offer price relative to value metrics based on industry peer price multiples, Zheng discusses some possible problems in the valuation methodology and finds that IPOs are not overvalued and do not underperform their industry peers in the five years after IPO.

4

Intermediaries in the IPO Process

In this section, we first investigate the methods used to set the price during the IPO (auction, fixed price, and bookbuilding), and concentrates on the role played by brokers and institutional investors. Since valuation is a hard and crucial step of the IPO process, companies going public hire one or more investment banks that are in charge, among many other tasks, to set the price at which shares will be offered to investors. However, agency problems often arise between issuers and underwriters, with underwriters being pushed to act in a way that is not fully aligned with the issuer's interests. The cause of these agency problems mainly lies in the remuneration mechanisms of IPO underwriters in exchange for the services they provide to companies that decide to list.

"Google is not a conventional company. We do not intend to become one." With these words extracted from the "Letter from the Founders" attached to the Google IPO prospectus, one of its two founders, Larry Page, justifies the choice of an anomalous IPO mechanism. From many points of view, in effect the Google IPO on the Nasdaq (IPO market cap of 23 billion dollars) on August 19, 2004 displays unique characteristics, a few of them being: an offering via an online Dutch auction, financial intermediaries playing a minor role, the presence of many underwriters

(31), underwriting fees lower than the average (2.75% compared to the traditional "7% solution"), and share allocation being at issuer's discretion.

Following this "anomalous" flotation, the lively debate on offering methodologies has been particularly rekindled in recent years. Historically speaking, three alternative main offering methods can be identified, all of them being largely investigated by scholars:

(a) the auction mechanism;

(b) fixed price offer;

(c) the bookbuilding procedure.

In the auction mechanism, competitive bids are invited for the IPO and are used as the basis for choosing the shares allocation and the offer price. Several authors have re-evaluated this method which has only spread to a few countries such as France and Japan during the preceding decades. On the other hand, fixed price offers were used internationally up to the end of the 1980s, except for the USA and Canada. This methodology was indeed the method most frequently used until the bookbuilding procedure was adopted by nearly all the share markets.

Bookbuilding spread in Europe when a sweeping program of privatization was begun by the British government at the start of the 1980s needing very large companies to be floated on several international markets. It was this wave of privatization that brought about the adoption of the bookbuilding technique, which had only been used in the USA and Canada until then. This listing method makes the offering at a variable price set within a price-range indicated in the prospectus (which may or may not be binding for the price set). Once the demand for the share offering has been tested by examining the demand from institutional investors, the offering price is defined.

According to several academic articles, the reason underlying the international acceptance of bookbuilding is the greater control and flexibility it guarantees (Ljungqvist, 2009; Ritter and Welch, 2002; Wilhelm, 2005). Nevertheless, the financial press often feels that the auction mechanism provides investors with greater benefits and blames its scarce use on the negotiating power of the large investment banks. The academic research does not agree on this subject. Several authors are convinced that bookbuilding is inadequate and suggest new auction methods should be adopted (Ausubel, 2002; Biais and Faugeron-Crouzet, 2002; Bulow and Klemperer, 2002; Derrien and Womack, 2003). Strengthened in this conviction, the top theoretical researchers into auctions have recently founded a company (Market Design Inc.) to develop an optimal auction design for the various markets, including IPOs. However, there are numerous theoretical models and empirical evidence for the validity of bookbuilding. For example, Jagannathan and Sherman (2006) show that infrequent recourse to auctions cannot be attributed to investor unfamiliarity with this mechanism only, nor differences in underwriting fees. Furthermore, in contrast to what happens in auctions of Treasury bonds, IPOs are not launched with regularity and those who attend auctions vary substantially from IPO to IPO, and the valuation of the offer price itself contains more elements of criticality. As much as adopting network technology can undoubtedly facilitate auctions, the risk still remains that auctions are rarely efficient when it is difficult to acquire information (Sherman, 2005). In fact, the incentive to collect and analyze information on the company going public is one of the components in theoretical models in support of the bookbuilding procedure. For example, Benveniste and Spindt (1989) as well as Maksimovic and Pichler (2001) argue that underpricing is itself a mechanism to persuade investors to reveal relevant information. Similarly, Sherman and Titman (2002) model underpricing as an instrument used by investors to repay the cost of acquiring information. In fact, the phenomenon of underpricing is often viewed as a failure of bookbuilding to guarantee that the supply of share offerings will meet the demand. Nevertheless, a reduction in underpricing is not unequivocally associated with auctions compared to bookbuilding: although Derrien and Womack (2003) found less underpricing in auctions, Wilhelm (2005) does not generally agree, highlighting that neither the traditional auction (referring to the French market) nor the more recent experiments show lower levels of underpricing.

Table 4.1 summarizes the advantages and disadvantages of the three techniques used to set the price.

Table 4.1: Advantages and disadvantages of mechanisms to price IPOs

Mechanism of Price Setting	Advantages	Disadvantages
The auction mechanism	• Price fixed in a "competitive" way • Less discrimination between the various investors • Greater benefits for investors	• Investors are not familiar with this mechanism • Investment in an IPO is not "standard" • The company is unsure about how much capital will be raised • Investors are uncertain of offering price • Underwriters may oppose it
Fixed price offer	• No uncertainty about the final IPO price	• Greater risk of the offering failing
The bookbuilding procedure	• The willingness of investors to pay is evaluated more easily • Compared to auctions, investors usually have larger guarantees on offer price	• Investment banks and institutional investors have greater negotiating power

In addition to the offering methodology, the debate on the efficiency of the primary market concerns the share allocation technique. The IPO share allocation traditionally favors institutional investors (Hanley and Wilhelm, 1995; Ljungqvist and Wilhelm, 2002), with the evidence covering all the major stock markets. On the other hand, the question debated concerns the allocation method that may guarantee the underwriter total discretion as in the USA, or alternatively can be limited by the regulation as in European markets. In other words, the open question is whether or not the efficiency of the markets benefits from a discretionary form of IPO share allocation. On the one hand, discretion means underwriters can remunerate clients who reveal more information.

In fact, in the absence of discretion in the allocation, the risk is that incentives for investors to compete in the bookbuilding phase will not be provided. Without some form of compensation, such as a larger allocation of discounted shares (underpricing), institutional investors would have little incentive to reveal truthful signs of interest in an IPO, conscious of the fact that such a demonstration of interest might only lead to a rise in the issue price without any profit for the investor. Indiscriminate allocation of shares at the IPO would therefore be incompatible with the principle of informational efficiency (Benveniste and Spindt, 1989). On the other hand, there is the risk that conflicts of interest will arise out of the discretion in the share allocation. In fact, the difference between "discretionary" and "discriminatory" forms of allocation is slight and the discretionary allocation mechanism can be used as an instrument for discriminatory price policies. Consequently, the discretionary element may aggravate the problem of agency between the issuer and offering bank because the bank interacts more often with institutional clients (repeated game) and less often with the issuer (Baron, 1982). This could be a precursor to collusion between banks and institutional investors (Biais *et al.*, 2002).

In terms of empirical proof, Ljungqvist and Wilhelm (2002) verify that the imposition of limits on the discretionary allocation induces offer prices more guided by the price ranges published in prospectuses. The authors interpret this evidence as a sign that production of information has contracted: the offer price does not exceed the limits initially fixed because there is little incentive to gather new information on the IPO company. Jenkinson *et al.* (2006) study the definition of offer price in relation to price range published in the prospectus and note the following relationships: more than half American IPOs have an offer price outside the initial price range, while listings with a price outside the price range are decidedly rare in Europe.

The reason for this difference could lie in the differing regulations concerning the communication of information. While in the USA any form of communication by the issuing company with the market is forbidden until the publication of the prospectus (and therefore the price range), in Europe the exchange of information between investors and underwriters has normally already taken place before the setting of the price range. Therefore, in the light of information already gathered by the market, European IPO underwriters determine a more trustworthy price range. The presence of a commitment by the underwriter not to exceed the maximum limit of the price range is compatible with the incentive for investors to indicate their liking. In fact, since indicative requests have already been received in Europe before the setting of the price range, the investors, fearing a rise in price, will be excessively cautious in exposing themselves in the request if it is not suitably guaranteed. This guarantee is accompanied by a simultaneous commitment of the underwriting banks not to exceed the price range independently from the market feedback, and not to favor the institutions in the case of oversubscription. The latter threat is aimed at inducing the institutions to declare truthfully during the bookbuilding phase, on pain of being excluded from the offering if they underestimate their indicated level of interest, which the underwriter uses to set the price range.

In this way, Jenkinson *et al.* (2006) highlight that not only the initial return (underpricing) but also the choice of the price range plays a strategic role in the incentive to extract information. On the other hand, Field and Lowry (2009) concentrate on the role of institutional investors in IPOs. If the performance of the newly listed company is not as good as the market benchmark (see the next paragraph on long-run underperformance), why is it that institutional investors are attracted in such large numbers? The authors explain that institutional investors can discern ex-ante which IPOs are being offered by good quality companies. In fact, not all IPOs are poor investments and the best perform exceptionally well (even over 1000% in three years). The challenge for the institutions is therefore to identify those new listings that will then guarantee excellent returns. To do this, the institutions invest time in gathering knowledge by, for instance, attending the road-show. Furthermore, according to several authors, their advantage compared to public retail lies in very close links with other actors in the IPO process who are better informed, such as venture capital companies and the underwriters themselves. In this situation, a repeated game could be set in motion in which institutional clients obtain information from underwriters and also provide information to the underwriters. If the institutional investors could enjoy an informational advantage in new listings, this category of investor would therefore be in a position to select the best IPOs. By coherently following this conjecture, the authors prove that company IPOs subscribed to by many institutional clients perform better post-IPO.

Analyzing the strategies of IPO share allocation is a promising research topic for the future, but data are not publicly available and this limits the opportunity for empirical research.

The structure of an IPO also includes the decision to offer newly issued shares rather than sell existing shares. The offer may be mostly composed of new issue shares (primary shares), with the capital raised flowing into the company. On the other hand, if the IPO is made through secondary shares (offering of existing shares) the operation only affects the company's ownership structure, which shows a change in the shareholding group without any monetary benefits arising for the company itself. Indeed, offering existing shares leads to the listing of pre-existing shares on the secondary share market, which are generally owned by shareholders who view the IPO as an opportunity to disinvest or diversify. An empirical approach to the theme has been proposed by Huyghebaert and Van Hulle (2006) who studied the factors determining the proportion of shares in the IPO offered on the primary and the secondary markets. They find that companies that at the IPO are younger, smaller, and with a high market-to-book ratio have usually a high proportion of newly issued shares. The proportion of newly issued shares offered is not related to company leverage, but depends on the level of bank debt: companies with more bank debt have a larger proportion of primary shares. External factors beyond the company's control, the trends in market indices, or the number of companies going public on the market the year up to the listing do not seem to influence the structure of the IPO, whether composed of primary or secondary shares. IPOs with a large proportion of newly issued shares have a greater tendency to increase capital in the years immediately following the IPO. This evidence is consistent with the hypothesis that flotations involving the issue of new shares are often a premise to company growth. The probability of being subject to takeover is greater for IPOs composed of a larger proportion of secondary shares. Consequently, the transfer of shares by the existing IPO shareholding group may be interpreted as the first sign of a disinvestment strategy that can later lead to the transfer of control of the company.

5

Short- and Long-Run Performance

This section focuses on the IPO phenomena which are interpreted as financial market "anomalies". In fact, in the short-term, the tendency worldwide is to show the first-day price above the offer price. This phenomenon (namely underpricing) attracts a great deal of attention from academics, and, although interpretative models on this subject are many, there is still no clear agreed answer in the literature as to which are the reasons for the increase in price at the first day of listing. Traditionally, empirical studies find that in the long term newly listed companies tend to perform below the market benchmark, both operationally and in terms of stock prices. The question generally debated is the following: do financial markets evaluate the listing of new IPO companies efficiently, or is the IPO selectively affected by adverse market anomalies and/or associated phenomena?

For sure, a company IPO will significantly change the shareholding structure. A new type of investor forms part of the company's capital, one who is not directly connected with the running of the company and who only expects suitable remuneration from their investment. Consequently a significant proportion of the literature studying new IPO companies analyses the trend in the relevant share price. In particular, attention is concentrated on two aspects:

(a) comparison between the price on the first day of trading and the offer price;

(b) comparison of long-run performance (3–5 years) with that of a benchmark.

The phenomenon of underpricing affects the first of these two points, that is, there is normally a positive difference between the first-day price and the offer price, while the second aspect is often a case of those who invest in new IPO offerings and keep the shares long enough obtaining a lower return on the investment compared to what they would have enjoyed by investing in the market portfolio. Underpricing leads to "old" shareholders transferring wealth to the new, choosing a price below the equilibrium market price, and so "money left on the table" is spoken of. There is a very articulate debate over explanations of this "anomaly" and there are various contributors who, without abandoning the market efficiency hypothesis, justify the frequent occurrence of underpricing. *Vice versa*, given the inferior performance of IPO-firms compared to investing in a portfolio of listed companies with similar characteristics, long-run performance shows that the price chosen by the old shareholders to persuade investors to buy shares during the IPO may not be a fair price. The literature does not provide a convincing explanation of this second anomaly. Moreover, the methodological problems associated with analyzing long-run performance make it even more difficult to evaluate the various markets.

In addition to these two aspects, the literature has recently focused on two other peculiarities in post-IPO performance. Firstly, on average the operating results deteriorate post-IPO (post-issue operating under-performance), and secondly, the survival rate is analyzed, that is to say, the tendency of the new-IPO companies to experience a higher rate of delisting than the market average.

5.1 Underpricing

Underpricing in various international markets is studied in the economic-financial literature, and during the various periods analyzed it has been found that on average the subscription of shares in newly listed companies and their resale on the secondary market on the first day of negotiation generates a positive return (Loughran *et al.*, 1994). To explain this anomaly most of the theories consider the underpricing to be a rational equilibrium reached as a solution in the prevailing market conditions. Without refuting the efficiency of the stock market, several theoretical models have been developed based on asymmetric information between the various subjects involved in the listing process. So the underpricing originates in asymmetrical information so that the IPO is "discounted" to compensate the less informed category.

The theoretical approaches to explaining underpricing therefore fall into the following categories:

(a) asymmetric information between issuing companies and the investors;

(b) asymmetric information between issuing companies and the underwriters;

(c) asymmetric information between various types of investors;

(d) theories based on the hypothesis of asymmetric information between various participants.

Theories based on asymmetric information between issuing companies and investors expect issuers to be more informed than investors, or vice versa. In the former case, not being able to discern the quality IPOs, the investors are reluctant to get involved in the market as they fear they will generate a "market for lemons" for themselves in which only companies of below-average quality go public. The quality issuers are therefore persuaded to go public underpriced to signal their quality (signaling theory: in terms of quality, underpricing is a costly signal). The cost of underpricing is recovered after the IPO, for instance through seasoned offers, thanks to the efficiency of the market in valuing companies of good quality (Allen and Faulhaber, 1989; Chemmanur, 1993; Welch, 1989). Similarly, the issuing company (and the relevant underwriter) can use underpricing as an instrument to guarantee good demand for the shares after the flotation thanks to the underpricing offered to the investors to leave "a good taste in investors' mouths" (Ibbotson, 1975).

On the other hand, if the investor is more informed than the issuer, for example, should he or she be more knowledgeable about the market demand for shares, underpricing is an instrument (monetary premium) the issuing company uses to test demand for the share issue. In other words, for investors underpricing is a monetary reward for releasing information on their ability to pay (information revelation theories). This assumption has recently given rise to a plethora of interpretations not only of the underpricing phenomenon but more generally of the offering and share allocation methodology, and the role brokers play in these (see the previous paragraph which discusses offering methodology).

Another situation of asymmetric information involves issuing companies and underwriters. From the point of view taken by the agency cost theory, instead of the issuer being less informed than the investor, the issuer may be less informed than the underwriter. This brings about a conflict of interest between issuer-underwriter-investors with underpricing being interpreted as a concession made by the issuing company to persuade underwriters to make a greater effort to deal with the share offering (Baron, 1982). Schenone (2004) empirically verifies that the existence of a relationship between the issuing company and the underwriting bank preceding the IPO is associated with a reduction in underpricing. So a possible interpretation is that this particular issuer-underwriter relationship reduces asymmetric information and leads to a more favorable evaluation of the company which in turn translates into a lower level of underpricing.

Furthermore, underpricing can be explained within a framework of asymmetric information between investors: different categories of investors are informed in different ways, and in order for the less informed to participate in the subscription, an offering premium is required (the underpricing). The first of these theories is the "winner's curse" suggested by Rock (1986). Two categories of investors can be identified: firstly, informed investors able to discern quality IPOs, and secondly, the uninformed. The latter are subject to adverse selection, having full access to overpriced IPOs deserted by the informed investors, and the rationing of the quality IPOs is also shared with the informed investors (partial allocation). So an equilibrium is developed which does not exclude the uninformed from participating, so that the underpricing becomes a necessary pre-condition to persuade uninformed investors to participate in the market.

Indeed, without the initial underpricing, the expected return for private investors would be negative as these investors would not be able to discern the quality new issues, so it is highly likely that they would buy the "bad" issues and not the "good" ones. On the other hand, the strategy of buying new issues and reselling them during the first day of listing has a significantly positive performance for institutional investors. The latter manages to obtain higher quotes for high-quality IPOs thanks to their greater ability to distinguish quality new issues, while they discharge issues of modest quality.

The asymmetric information between investors can also persuade those less informed to condition their purchase requests to the behavior of the other investors, implicitly considered to be more informed. This assumption underpins the theory of informational cascade proposed by Welch (1992). Individual investors judge how much interest there is in the IPO from other investors and then request subscription to hot IPOs. Consequently, issuing companies discount their offer price in order to attract initial investors who in turn induce a cascade of further requests to subscribe. To this extent, underpricing serves to limit the risk of an unsuccessful IPO due to a lack of subscriptions. An interesting empirical study validating this theory has been put forward by Amihud et al. (2003) in that IPOs are generally either undersubscribed or hugely oversubscribed and only moderately oversubscribed in extremely rare exceptions.

Lastly, theories based on asymmetric information have enjoyed less attention recently. Here the legal liability theory (Hughes and Thakor, 1992; Tinic, 1988) is cited, in which underpricing is an instrument used to reduce the probability of legal action, and the theory based on trading commissions according to which underpricing is a means used by the underwriter to stimulate post-IPO transactions and therefore to negotiate additional margins during the aftermarket (Boehmer and Fishe, 2001).

Table 5.1 presents a summary of studies on IPO underpricing, published in entrepreneurship, management and finance journals.

5.2   Long-Run Underperformance

Companies tend to perform below the market benchmark during the first few years after the IPO. This anomaly was identified for the first time by Ritter (1991) and has so far carried out in numerous international studies. More recently, starting with Jain and Kini (1994), the literature points even to a post-issue underperformance in terms of operating measures. The explanations put forward for this phenomenon revolve around three main theories (Khurshed *et al.*, 2003):

(a) theories of market timing;

(b) theories of window dressing;

(c) theories of asymmetric information.

The first explains underperformance in terms of a timing decision in entering the market, be that timing "exogenous" or "endogenous" to the company being floated. One of the exogenous reasons is the theory of window of opportunity (Loughran and Ritter, 1995) according to which companies go public (or in general raise equity capital) not when the growth prospects are good and so financing is required, but when the controlling shareholder finds it optimal. The incentive to go public is particularly strong in periods when a specific sector is relatively overvalued. Think, for instance, of the Internet bubble at the end of the 1990s or the recent consideration reserved for the energy market. Otherwise, the market timing may originate endogenously in the issuing company so that it is inclined to go public at a time of maximum performance, that is when it is able to take advantage of favorable valuation by the market. According to Yang *et al.* (2011), the executives' track record has a significant impact on the choice of the IPO timing.

Similarly, the theory of window dressing is based on this consideration, according to which before the IPO companies are subject to

Table 5.1: Literature on IPO underpricing

Authors	Journal	Key Findings
Arthurs et al. (2009)	Journal of Business Venturing	To reduce information asymmetries for potential investors considering investment in an IPO venture, owners can signal the firm's longer-term viability and quality in several ways. The lockup period is one signal that can be offered. This paper investigates the lockup period of a sample of 640 ventures going through the IPO and finds that a longer lockup period acts as a substitute signal to venture capital (VC) and prestigious underwriter backing. Furthermore, the paper proved that ventures which have a going concern issue can reduce the amount of underpricing at the time of the IPO by accepting a longer lockup period.
Boeh and Dunbar (2016)	Journal of Financial Economics	This study examines how initial public offering (IPO) pricing is affected by the pipeline of deals in registration, measured at the underwriter level. Examining IPOs from 2002 to 2013, the authors find evidence that measures of the IPO bookrunner's pipeline significantly affect pricing decisions. The evidence is mostly consistent with market power and agency theories, which argue that underwriters use a young or growing pipeline to push for higher IPO first day returns.
Boulton et al. (2010)	Journal of International Business Studies	It is well established that a link exists between a country's legal system and the size, liquidity, and value of its capital markets. The authors of this paper study how differences in country-level governance affect the underpricing of initial public offerings (IPOs). Examining 4,462 IPOs across 29 countries from 2000 to 2004, they find the surprising result that underpricing is higher in countries with corporate governance that strengthens the position of investors relative to insiders. They conjecture that when countries give outsiders more influence, IPO issuers underprice more to generate excess demand for the offer, which in turn leads to greater ownership dispersion and reduces outsiders' incentives to monitor the behavior of corporate insiders. In other words, underpricing is a cost that insiders pay to maintain control in countries with legal systems designed to empower outsiders. Consistent with this control motivation for underpricing, they find that underpricing has a negative association with post-IPO outside blockholdings and a positive association with private control benefits. In addition, firms whose insiders are entrenched either by majority ownership or by dual-class structures do not underprice more in countries with better governance. In these firms the ownership structure protects managers from outside influence, eliminating the incentive to increase outside ownership dispersion through underpricing.

Continued.

Table 5.1: Continued

Authors	Journal	Key Findings
Boulton *et al.* (2013)	Journal of Finance	The initial public offerings (IPOs) of diversified firms, those reporting more than one business segment at the time they go public, experience less underpricing than do IPOs by focused issuers. The authors explore two explanations for this phenomenon. Diversification may benefit IPO firms by reducing information asymmetries and therefore lowering underpricing costs. Alternatively, high quality focused firms may be signaling their value by underpricing their shares to a greater degree. Though they find at least some evidence consistent with each explanation, a majority of the evidence favors signaling.
Boulton *et al.* (2017)	Journal of International Business Studies	The authors of this paper study the impact of country-level accounting conservatism on international IPO underpricing. Examining 13,285 IPOs from 36 countries, they find that IPOs are underpriced less in countries in which existing public firms practice more accounting conservatism. The link between conservatism and underpricing is robust to alternative measures of conservatism, country mean regressions, sample country exclusions, and endogenous treatment models. Consistent with the hypothesis that conservatism reduces underpricing by mitigating the impact of information asymmetries, they find that higher country-level conservatism is associated with lower country-level PIN values and that the negative relation between conservatism and underpricing is strongest for IPOs involving small firms in which information asymmetries are likely to be high. Lastly, they find evidence that legal origin, a factor linked to the practice of conservatism, influences the relations between underpricing and conservatism.
Daily *et al.* (2003)	Entrepreneurship Theory and Practice	Initial public offerings (IPOs) have been a prominent focus of academic and popular press attention, especially in recent years. Much of this attention can be attributed to the increase in IPO activity as a function of the "dot com" phenomenon. Of particular interest to both academics and practitioners is IPO underpricing. Review of existing research suggests little consensus regarding those factors associated with underpricing. The authors of this paper provide a meta analysis of published studies. Their findings reveal a number of significant relationships, many of which are opposite to the predictions offered by the signaling theory. Implications of these findings for practice and future research are discussed.

Continued.

Table 5.1: Continued

Authors	Journal	Key Findings
Daily *et al.* (2005)	Journal of Business Venturing	In this study, the authors examine those factors generally considered to impact IPO performance to assess the extent to which investment bankers might utilize this information in determining the spread within which the offering price is likely to be set and in setting the offering price. Interestingly, they find no evidence that the variables investigated are related to either IPO offer price spread or the IPO offer price. The implications of these findings are notable, as they raise the issue of what information might account for investment bankers' valuation decisions, as captured in the offer price spread and offer price.
Judge *et al.* (2015)	Strategic Management Journal	Prior studies of IPO underpricing, mostly using agency theory and single-country samples, have generally fallen short. In this study, the authors employ the knowledge-based view (KBV) to explore underpricing across 17 countries. They find that agency indicators are insignificant predictors, board of director knowledge limits underpricing, and external knowledge both substitutes for and complements internal board knowledge. This third finding suggests that future KBV studies should consider how internal and external knowledge states interact with each other. This study offers new insights into the antecedents of underpricing and extends our understanding of comparative governance and the KBV of the firm.
Kaur and Singh (2015)	Management and Labour Studies	India has been endeavoring to achieve gender equality, but has failed to attain much success in the corporate sector. The male-dominated Indian corporate board clearly exhibits gender discrimination. The much-awaited move has finally come from the Indian legislators who took an audacious step towards gender egalitarianism by mandating women directors in Indian boardrooms with the advent of New Companies Act, 2013. The scenario of women involvement on Indian boards just prior to this enactment has been appraised through this study. A glimpse on the advantages accruing to the companies permitting women-led initial public offering (IPO) is explored. The impact of the presence of women directors on IPO underpricing is examined by analyzing 230 Indian companies that went public from May 1, 2007 to March 31, 2013. It was found that more than 50% of the sample companies lack gender diversity and in fact employ no women directors in their boards. The results point towards the existence of women on Indian boards as mere token who fail to impede IPO underpricing. The implication for the managers of Indian companies is to pursue the global trend of female inclusion and appraise women on Indian boards from mere tokens to form a critical mass to procure the benefits of gender diversity.

Continued.

Table 5.1: Continued

Authors	Journal	Key Findings
Li *et al.* (2016)	Journal of Accounting and Economics	The authors of this paper investigate the extent to which capitalization of expected capital gains taxes and the lock-in effect induced by the capital gains tax rate differential simultaneously impact the pricing and underpricing of initial public offerings (IPOs). Using a large sample of IPOs from 1987 to 2010, they estimate regressions of offer prices and first-day underpricing on tax rates. Supporting tax capitalization, IPO offer prices decrease in long-term capital gains taxes. Supporting lock-in, IPO underpricing increases in the long-term and short-term tax rate differential. These effects are consistent with capital gains taxes simultaneously reducing IPO proceeds and exacerbating IPO underpricing.
Lowry and Murphy (2007)	Journal of Financial Economics	In about one-third of US IPOs between 1996 and 2000, executives received stock options with an exercise price equal to the IPO offer price rather than a market-determined price. Among firms with such "IPO options", 58% of top executives realize a net benefit from underpricing: the gain from the options exceeds the loss from the dilution of their pre-IPO shareholdings. If executives can influence either the IPO offer price or the timing and terms of their stock option grants, there should be a positive relation between IPO option grants and underpricing. The authors find no evidence of such a relation. The results contrast sharply with the emerging literature on managerial self-dealing at shareholder expense.
Morricone *et al.* (2017)	Research Policy	This paper studies the interplay between two defining features of technology-based firms: licensing as a commercialization strategy and the reliance on equity financing. Within the context of an IPO, the authors argue that the technology commercialization strategy of a firm going public affects information asymmetries and, therefore, IPO underpricing. In particular, they theorize that underpricing will be higher when a firm's technology commercialization strategy is more based on licenses. They also posit that the size of the patent portfolio will mitigate this effect. Their results from a sample of 130 IPOs in the US semiconductor industry confirm these predictions.

Continued.

Table 5.1: Continued

Authors	Journal	Key Findings
Park and Patel (2015)	Journal of Management Studies	The authors explore the relationship between ambiguity, or low information clarity, in the IPO prospectus of newly public firms and their underpricing. Consistent with signaling theory, they find that IPO underpricing is low when the prospectus contains less ambiguous information that creates a more reliable signal conveying the quality of the IPO firm. However, the positive association between ambiguity and IPO underpricing is less pronounced when IPO firms display low strategic conformity with other firms in the industry, operate in industries with high valuation heterogeneity, or are medium-sized. Using a sample of 398 IPOs between 1998 and 2007, the results support these predictions. This study shows the importance of the signaling environment influencing boundedly rational signal recipients interpreting ambiguous signals.
Wang and Wan (2013)	Strategic Entrepreneurship Journal	In this study, the authors argue from the resource-based view and multiple agency theory that private and corporate VC firms have different impacts on IPO underpricing among VC-backed IPOs due to their different interests, motivations, and resources. Private VC firms are primarily financial oriented, but corporate VC firms generally are strategic in orientation. Using a sample of 200 VC-backed IPOs from 2000 to 2007, they found support for the hypotheses that among VC-backed IPOs, private VC ownership is positively associated with underpricing, whereas corporate VC ownership is negatively associated with underpricing.
Willenborg et al. (2015)	Journal of Accounting Research	The authors study the relation between issuer operating performance and initial public offering (IPO) price formation from the initial price range to the offer price to the closing price on the first trading day. For a post-bubble sample of 2001–2013 IPOs, they find that pre-IPO net income and, in particular, operating cash flow are strongly, positively associated with the revision from the mid-point of the initial price range to the offer price and that the "partial adjustment phenomenon" concentrates among issuers with the strongest operating performance. As for why publicly observable information helps predict changes in valuation from when the initial price range is set to when the offer price is set, their findings suggest that strong-performing issuers, especially those offering small slices of ownership, have lower bargaining incentives and are susceptible to the underwriter(s) low-balling the price range. Overall, their results suggest an important role for accounting information in understanding the pricing of book-built IPOs and are consistent with the presence of agency problems between issuers and underwriters.

strong incentives to "embellish" their balance sheet and may engage in creative accounting (earning management) which leads to greater pre-IPO profitability than cannot be maintained post-issue. This results in a deteriorating post-issue operational performance due to a simple mean reversion effect (Fama, 1998). In turn, the market recognizes it valued the company with excessive optimism at the IPO and consequently the share prices decline (Teoh *et al.*, 1998). A similar assumption is introduced by Benson *et al.* (2015), according to which companies with shareholder-unfriendly provisions—such as, for example, staggered boards or supermajority voting—are inclined to "camouflage" this fact at the IPO by using more obscure, harder-to-parse language.

The third reason for long-run underperformance arises out of the theory of asymmetric information that speaks of opportunism (moral hazard) derived from the change in ownership structure at the time of the IPO. Indeed, the decision to go public increases agency costs by dispersing the share ownership. So it changes the relationship between the principal (shareholders) and agent (manager). The decline in performance could therefore be caused by both an ex-ante effect of adverse selection (Leland and Pyle, 1977) by companies which decide to go public, and by the ex-post effect of opportunistic behavior (Jensen and Meckling, 1976) such as the company management pursuing private benefits once being public (perquisite consumption) or the underwriters allocating more IPO shares to retail investors when they expect poor long-run performance and to institutional investors when expectations are more optimistic (Bonaventura *et al.*, 2018).

Finally, a fourth possible reason underlying long-run performance is the structure of the share offering. In fact, hypothesizing heterogeneous expectations about the value of the company, only optimistic investors subscribe IPO shares. The valuation converges on market expectations in the after-market, and the price consequently falls.

According to theories of market timing, companies go public to maximize returns for existing shareholders when their sector is "optimistically" valued by the market (windows of opportunity), or companies go public at the time of maximum performance to take advantage of favorable market valuations (window dressing). Prior to the IPO, companies make their balance sheets "shine" through the use of "creative accounting" practices (earning management).

In recent years, research on long-run performance has concentrated to provide international empirical evidence, into the methodological problems connected with measuring post-IPO performance. In fact, the anomaly of long-run underperformance is not perceived as such by all the academic community, and its study could become one of the most controversial topics in the IPO literature during the next few years (Ritter and Welch, 2002). On the one hand, researchers like Ritter and Welch see a market anomaly in the post-IPO performance investigated using instruments of behavioral finance, and on the other hand, there are "efficientist" authors such as Fama and French who put the theory of efficiency forward in the form of semi-strong efficient markets. For these researchers the evidence of long-run underperformance is caused by specification errors in the models used to measure it. Actually, *per se*, all efficiency tests such as those of performance are at the same time a test of the efficiency of the market and a test of the efficiency of the model used. The position taken by "efficientists" on the empirical evidence for long-run underperformance is not that it is a real market anomaly but that it represents a methodological problem such as, for instance, a failure to consider the risk level, or a survival bias. Furthermore, there can be methodological problems in defining what the benchmark is. Traditionally a market index has been adopted as the benchmark, but the hypothesis is that small and medium-sized firms perform worse than others. It can therefore be argued that since newly listed companies are generally small or medium-sized enterprises, their relative underperformance does not result from the recent IPO but simply from the fact they are smaller in size.

In more general terms, the hypothesis of efficiency is based on the idea of perfect rationality, which has recently been thrown into doubt by models of behavioral finance. This is based on evidence in behavioral psychology concerning irrationality (or at least limited rationality) in the way individuals perceive the situation and react to it. There are various sources of judgement bias. For example, an irrational investor attitude towards risk: individuals confronted with risky alternatives show more interest in minimizing losses than maximizing profits. This hypothesis is derived from the theory of information which states that losses are perceived more forcefully than profits (Thaler, 1980; Tversky and Kahneman, 1981). Furthermore, investor irrationality may be expressed in how the probability of possible future events is evaluated. In identifying possible future results, subjects often tend to base their judgment on the recent past, assuming that this can be similar to what will happen in the immediate future. In other words, they overestimate recent information and underestimate more remote information from periods preceding the recent past (Kahneman and Tversky, 1982).

Lastly, in several studies company performance is related to the survival profile. For instance, Fama and French (2004) posit that the evidence for "poor" performance after the offering and for a recent increase in the rate of delisting in the years immediately following IPOs is due to a change in the nature of the companies floated. This change is explained by a decrease in the cost of capital for newly listed companies, which allows a weaker company to join the stock markets. Therefore, the market now evaluates companies of a different risk type and profile than those already floated on the market. Consequently, the tendency is for underperformance in the aftermarket to be associated with an increase in the frequency of delistings. In identifying variables able to predict the probability of surviving post listing, Peristiani and Hong (2004) found that good pre-IPO profitability is essential for a company to remain on the stock market post-IPO. Furthermore, Demers and Joos (2005) find a negative correlation between the probability of delisting and the underwriter's prestige ranking and the age of the company at IPO, while the relationship with venture capitalists is not significant. In contrast, Fan and Yamada (2020) and Chou *et al.* (2013) find that the presence and past track record of a venture capitalist before the IPO are determinants of the follow-up survival and performance. Michel (2014) introduces the possibility that the IPO long-run performance is impacted by the return of pre-IPO VC investments.

Jain and Kini (2004) demonstrate that a high level of investments in research and development and a good degree of industry diversification of investments can increase the likelihood of surviving on the market, while Chen *et al.* (2018) show that subsidies from public entities to IPO companies impact on the long-run performance.

Table 5.2 presents a summary of studies on the long-run performance of IPO-firms, published in entrepreneurship, management and finance journals.

Table 5.2: Literature on the long-run performance of IPOs

Authors	Journal	Key Findings
Benson *et al.* (2015)	Journal of Business Venturing	Entrepreneurs attempt to persuade potential investors that their new ventures are both credible and worthy of funding. A long line of research on entrepreneurial impression management establishes that the ability to present their ventures in a favorable light is a key attribute of successful entrepreneurs. This study examines the opposite side of the issue and tests if some entrepreneurs obscure corporate governance information. The authors create a new metric to measure the level of camouflage used in governance documents for initial public offerings (IPOs). They find that entrepreneurs are less likely to use camouflage during periods of high scrutiny, as measured by industry analyst following, industry concentration levels, and IPO clustering. The authors also find that greater use of camouflage is associated with raising more capital, due to both greater offer proceeds as well as less underpricing. This effect is most pronounced in corporate charters which are difficult for shareholders to change.
Bonardo *et al.* (2011)	Entrepreneurship Theory and Practice	Companies obtain significant benefits and resources from university affiliations. Building on recent contributions in organizational theory and signaling theory, the authors argue that such relationships redress investors' concerns over the legitimacy of firms and act as an uncertainty-reducing signal. They study the population of university spin-offs that have gone public in Europe over a decade, and find that academic affiliation reduces uncertainty and enhances the chances of survival in the long term, controlling for characteristics related to firm quality, including measures of intellectual and relational capital as well as corporate governance mechanisms. Thus, external stakeholders consider academic affiliation as a valuable and non-substitutable resource.
Brau *et al.* (2012)	Journal of Financial and Quantitative Analysis	The authors analyze 3,547 initial public offerings (IPOs) from 1985 through 2003 to determine the impact of acquisition activity on long-run stock performance. The results show that IPOs that acquire within a year of going public significantly underperform for 1- through 5-year holding periods following the 1st year, whereas nonacquiring IPOs do not significantly underperform over these time frames. For example, the mean 3-year style-adjusted abnormal return is −15.6% for acquirers and 5.9% for nonacquirers. Their cross-sectional and calendar-time results suggest that the acquisition activity of newly public firms plays an important and previously unrecognized role in the long-run underperformance of IPOs.

Continued.

Table 5.2: Continued

Authors	Journal	Key Findings
Bruton et al. (2010)	Strategic Management Journal	This paper examines performance effects of ownership concentration and two types of private equity investors (venture capitalists and business angels) in firms that have undergone an initial public offering (IPO) in the United Kingdom and France. The authors expand and contextualize nascent understanding of multiple agency theory by examining heterogeneity of private equity investors and by suggesting that multiple agency relationships are affected by different institutional contexts. They employ a unique, hand-collected dataset of 224 matched IPOs (112 in each country). Controlling for the endogeneity of private equity investors' retained share ownership, they find support for the agency theory argument that concentrated ownership improves IPOs' performance. The research also shows that the two types of private equity investors have a differential impact on performance, and the legal institutions in a given country moderate this impact.
Ecker (2014)	Contemporary Accounting Research	Due to a lack of an information history, IPO firms' information precision is not only generally low but also likely to be estimated initially with considerable error. The author of this paper finds that the deviation between expected and realized information precision is predictably associated with the magnitude and the persistence of long-run abnormal returns after an IPO. Specifically, an upward (downward) revision of information precision results in positive (negative) abnormal returns over the period in which investors update their beliefs. In addition, the positive abnormal returns of firms with unexpectedly high realized information precision are less persistent than the negative abnormal returns of firms with unexpectedly low realized information precision, which can extend up to 18 months after the IPO. The findings imply that long-term investors in IPO stocks do not necessarily behave irrationally, but that positive and negative post-IPO abnormal performance is also consistent with rational investors gradually updating the perceived information precision parameter of these stocks.
Ferris et al. (2013)	Review of Finance	Based on a textual analysis of initial public offering (IPO) prospectuses, the authors obtain a number of important findings regarding the relation between the conservatism in prospectuses, IPO pricing, and subsequent operating and stock return performance. First, prospectus conservatism is positively related to underpricing, with the relation more pronounced for technology than nontechnology firms. Second, for nontechnology IPOs, prospectus conservatism is able to predict the firm's post-IPO operating performance. Specifically, they find that conservatism is inversely related to the firm's post-IPO operating performance for the three years following the IPO. However, this predictability is limited to nontechnology IPOs. Finally, they find some evidence that for non-technology IPOs conservatism is inversely related to the firm's post-IPO abnormal stock return. They conclude that the conservatism contained in an IPO's prospectus reveals useful information about pricing and subsequent operating and stock return performance. Moreover, prospectus conservatism for nontechnology IPOs deserves more attention from investors.

Continued.

Table 5.2: Continued

Authors	Journal	Key Findings
How *et al.* (2011)	Australian Journal of Management	Dividend initiations are an economically significant event that has important implications for a firm's future financial capacity. Given the market's expectation of a consistent payout, managers of IPO firms must approach the initial dividend decision cautiously. The authors of this paper compare the long-run performance of IPO firms that initiated a dividend with that of similarly matched non-payers, and find robust results that firms which initiated a dividend perform significantly better up to five years after the initiation date. Further tests show that the post-initiation firm performance is explained mostly by dividend theory of signaling rather than free cash flow.
Jain and Tabak (2008)	Journal of Business Venturing	Despite the innate advantage founder CEOs have by virtue of their founding vision, organizational influence, positive image, and ownership stakes to lead their firms at their initial public offering (IPO), extant empirical evidence indicates that between a third to half of IPO firms go public with non-founder CEOs at the helm. Relatively little however, is known regarding factors that influence the choice of founder versus non-founder CEO for firms issuing IPOs. This study examines the impact of factors such as founder characteristics, size of founding team, governance structure, ownership structure, top management team independence, venture capitalist influence, and the demand for equity financing on the probability of founder CEO at IPO.
Jain *et al.* (2008)	Journal of Business Venturing	Extant empirical evidence indicates that the proportion of firms going public prior to achieving profitability has been increasing over time. This phenomenon is largely driven by an increase in the proportion of technology firms going public. Since there is considerable uncertainty regarding the long-term economic viability of these firms at the time of going public, identifying factors that influence their ability to attain key post-IPO milestones such as achieving profitability represents an important area of research. The authors employ a theoretical framework built around agency and signaling considerations to identify factors that influence the probability and timing of post-IPO profitability of Internet IPO firms. They estimate Cox Proportional Hazards models to test whether factors identified by the theoretical framework significantly impact the probability of post-IPO profitability as a function of time. They find that the probability of post-IPO profitability increases with pre-IPO investor demand and change in ownership at the IPO of the top officers and directors. On the other hand, the probability of post-IPO profitability decreases with the venture capital participation, proportion of outsiders on the board, and pre-market valuation uncertainty.

Continued.

Table 5.2: Continued

Authors	Journal	Key Findings
Jaskiewicz *et al.* (2005)	Family Business Review	This article examines the long-run stock market performance of German and Spanish initial public offerings (IPOs) between 1990 and 2000. The authors distinguish between family and nonfamily-owned business IPOs. Buy-and-hold-abnormal returns (BHAR) are computed in order to determine abnormal returns. Their results show that three years after going public, investors, on average, realized an abnormal return of −32.8% for German and −36.7% for Spanish IPOs. In both countries, nonfamily business IPOs perform insignificantly better. Regression analyses show that for the whole sample there is a positive company size effect. In family-owned businesses, strong family involvement has a positive impact on the long-run stock market performance, whereas the age of the firm has a negative influence.
Jia and Zhang (2014)	Journal of Management Studies	This study examines how stakeholders' investment time horizons interact with information about corporate giving in initial public offering (IPO) firms. Specifically, the authors build a model that explains how corporate philanthropy affects IPO performance. They find that at the IPO-preparation stage, corporate giving is negatively related to underwriter prestige, venture capital investment, and IPO financing costs. They also find that at the IPO-issuance stage, negative media coverage of IPOs moderates the U-shaped relationship between corporate giving and market premiums. At the IPO-trading stage, they find that corporate giving only positively influences the market premiums for IPO firms that are the subject of negative media reports. Their findings contribute to the signaling theory by showing how various stakeholders interpret the same signals differently, and they have implications for understanding how the relationship between corporate philanthropy and corporate financial performance materializes in the IPO markets.
Krishnan *et al.* (2011)	Journal of Financial and Quantitative Analysis	The authors examine the association of a venture capital (VC) firm's reputation with the post-initial public offering (IPO) long-run performance of its portfolio firms. They find that VC reputation, measured by the past market share of VC-backed IPOs, has significant positive associations with long-run firm performance measures. While more reputable VCs initially select better-quality firms, more reputable VCs continue to be associated with superior long-run performance, even after controlling for VC selectivity. They find that more reputable VCs exhibit more active post-IPO involvement in the corporate governance of their portfolio firms, and this continued VC involvement positively influences post-IPO firm performance.

Continued.

Table 5.2: Continued

Authors	Journal	Key Findings
Kroll *et al.* (2007)	Academy of Management Journal	Challenging agency theory prescriptions for board composition, this paper contends that the boards of young firms that have gone public are best comprised of a majority of original top management team (TMT) members, rather than independent outsiders. The authors argue that such board members possess valuable tacit knowledge of the firms and entrepreneurial visions and are in the best position to provide oversight. They additionally argue that outsiders should provide resources that firms' TMTs might use to execute their strategies, rather than monitor the TMTs. Their results from 1996–1997 data on 524 initial public offerings support the contentions.
Liu *et al.* (2014b)	Management Science	The unique characteristics of the US initial public offering (IPO) process, particularly the strict quiet period regulations, allow the authors to explore the effects of media coverage when the coverage does not contain genuine news (i.e., hard information that was previously unknown). They show that a simple, objective measure of pre-IPO media coverage is positively related to the stock's long-term value, liquidity, analyst coverage, and institutional investor ownership. Their results are robust to additional controls for size, to using abnormal or excess media, and to an instrumental variable approach. They also find that pre-IPO media coverage is negatively related to future expected returns, measured by the implied cost of capital. In all, they find a long-term role for media coverage, consistent with Merton's investor recognition hypothesis.
Michel (2014)	Entrepreneurship Theory and Practice	This paper examines the return on recent venture capital (VC) investment and its impact on the long-run stock market performance of initial public offerings (IPOs). Firms with higher return on recent VC investment underperform firms with lower return on recent VC investment by 32 to 43% in the 3-year period following the offer. This effect is robust to various risk-adjustment procedures. Market conditions at the time of the VC valuation and changes in these market conditions thereafter are the main drivers of this result, suggesting that investors are too optimistic or do not properly understand the informational content of the recent return on VC investment.

Continued.

Table 5.2: Continued

Authors	Journal	Key Findings
Moore *et al.* (2010)	Entrepreneurship Theory and Practice	In the current study, the authors develop an institutional embeddedness explanation of foreign initial public offering (IPO) performance. To explain the performance differentials of these firms, they investigate the effects of both "home" and "host" country institutional signals on IPO underpricing using a sample of foreign IPOs listed in two different institutional environments, namely, the US and UK stock exchanges. Supporting the view that signals are institutionally embedded and that their value is not universal, they find that the salience of signals associated with country of origin is contingent on the institutional environment of the listing exchange.
Mousa and Reed (2013)	Entrepreneurship Theory and Practice	Research on organization slack has focused mainly on its effect in large publicly traded firms, but little work exists on the value of slack resources for other firms. Therefore, this work addresses the question: Do slack resources matter in the case of initial public offerings (IPOs)? The authors argue that firms that possess financial, innovational, and managerial slack resources are sending a positive signal to potential investors regarding the quality of the IPO. Using a sample of high-tech IPOs, they find support for that contention.
Pandya (2016)	Jindal Journal of Business Research	Detailed review of literature in Indian and foreign context have empirically documented IPOs anomaly. This paper attempts to study immediate and short- to long-run performance of IPOs in India for the period January 2004 to December 2013. The present paper evaluates IPOs' performance from initial day to long-term period based on average abnormal return, cumulative abnormal return, buy and hold abnormal return, wealth relative, and market adjusted abnormal return. The paper concludes that IPOs are a good bet to rely upon from immediate to short run and at most till medium term.

Continued.

Table 5.2: Continued

Authors	Journal	Key Findings
Ragozzino and Reuer (2007)	Strategic Organization	Information asymmetries between buyers and sellers can create inefficiencies in mergers & acquisition (M&A) markets and prevent acquirers from gaining access to valuable resources and capabilities via acquisitions. Entrepreneurial firms face similar problems in raising external capital, due to the asymmetric information that separates them from prospective investors. In this article, the authors bring together the strategy, financial economics and entrepreneurship literatures and exploit the initial public offering (IPO) context to examine the informational characteristics of newly public entrepreneurial firms. They construct hazard models that offer strong evidence that certain IPO characteristics signal the value of entrepreneurial firms and thereby attract M&A suitors.
Reuer et al. (2012)	Academy of Management Journal	This article extends signaling theory to research on acquisition premiums and investigates the value that newly public targets capture in post-IPO acquisitions. The authors of this paper complement previous research on acquisition premiums by suggesting that signals about targets can enhance sellers' gains by reducing acquirers' offer price discounting that is due to information asymmetries. Specifically, they argue that target firms can engage in interorganizational relationships (e.g., associations with prominent investment banks, venture capitalists, and alliance partners) that function as signals and enhance sellers' gains. Empirical evidence shows that the benefits of such signals apply to domestic and cross-border deals alike and that these benefits are even greater for IPO targets selling their companies to acquirers based in different industries.
Smart et al. (2008)	Journal of Accounting and Economics	The authors of this paper find that relative to fundamentals, dual-class firms trade at lower prices than do single-class firms, both at the IPO and for at least the subsequent five years. The lower prices attached to duals do not foreshadow abnormally low stock or accounting returns. Moreover, some types of CEO turnover are less frequent among duals, and in general CEO turnover is sensitive to firm performance for singles but not for duals. Finally, when duals unify their share classes, statistically and economically significant value gains occur. Collectively, their results suggest that the governance associated with dual-class equity influences the pricing of duals.

Continued.

Table 5.2: Continued

Authors	Journal	Key Findings
Sundaramurthy et al. (2014)	Strategic Management Journal	This paper contributes to the corporate governance literature by developing and testing theory regarding positive and negative synergies between the CEO's and the board's human and social capital. Using a sample of 360 biotechnology firms that went public between 1995 and 2010, the authors demonstrate that accumulated public company board experiences of the CEO and the board have positive synergistic effects on IPO performance whereas the current board appointments have negative effects. While scientific educational backgrounds have positive synergies, industry specific experiences produce either positive or counterproductive effects depending on the age and profitability of the firm. Thus, this paper contributes to the corporate governance and human and social capital literatures by describing the costs and benefits of specific types and combinations of CEO and board capital.
Useche (2014)	Research Policy	This study investigates empirically whether patents can be signals to financial markets, thus reducing problems of asymmetric information. In particular the authors study how patenting behavior impacts on the way investors perceive software firms' growth potential through an increase in the amount invested at the initial public offering (IPO) of firms in the US and Europe. This study performs regressions on the relationship of patent applications before IPO and the amount of money collected at the IPO, while controlling other factors that may influence IPO performance. The authors also attempt to account for a potential source of endogeneity problems that can arise for self-selection bias and simultaneity between the number of patent applications prior to going public and the amount of money collected at IPO. They find significant and robust positive correlations between patent applications and IPO performance. The signaling power of patenting is significantly different for US and European companies, and is related to the difficulty in obtaining a signal and its scarcity. An additional patent application prior to IPO increases IPO proceeds by about 0.507% and 1.13% for US and European companies, respectively. Results suggest that a less 'applicant friendly' patenting system increases the credibility of patents as signals and their value for IPO investors.

Continued.

Table 5.2: Continued

Authors	Journal	Key Findings
Wagner and Cockburn (2010)	Research Policy	This paper analyzes the effect of patenting on the survival prospects of 356 Internet-related firms that made an initial public offering on the NASDAQ at the height of the stock market bubble of the late 1990s. By March 2005, almost 2/3 of these firms had delisted from the exchange. Changes in the legal environment in the US in the 1990s made it much easier to obtain patents on software, and ultimately, on business methods, though less than 1/2 of the firms in the sample obtained, or attempted to obtain, patents. For those that did, the authors hypothesize that patents conferred competitive advantages that translate into higher probability of survival, though they may also simply be a signal of firm quality. Controlling for other determinants of firm survival, patenting is positively associated with survival. Quite different processes appear to govern exit via acquisition compared to exit via delisting from the exchange due to business failure. Firms that applied for more patents were less likely to be acquired, though if they obtain unusually highly cited patents they may be a more attractive acquisition target. These findings do generally not hold true for "business method" patents, which do not appear to confer a survival advantage.
Weber and Willenborg (2003)	Journal of Accounting Research	Do expert informational intermediaries add value? This paper addresses this question by examining the informativeness of the audit report contained in the prospectus associated with a firm's IPO. At the time of the IPO, there is a relative lack of information to facilitate the establishment of equity values, suggesting that the information provided by outside "experts" (e.g., auditors, underwriters) is particularly important. In this article the authors study small, non-venture-backed IPOs, a segment of the market with the poorest long-run performance and where the prestigious audit firm is often the sole (if any) expert present. They find that the pre-IPO opinions of larger auditors are more predictive of post-IPO negative stock delistings. Of particular note, the opinions of the national-tiered firms are comparably predictive to those of the Big 6, though this finding emerges only after they consider the selectivity based differences in the clients that hire these national firms. The findings also indicate that, for larger auditors the presence of a pre-IPO going-concern opinion is more strongly associated with first-year stock returns and that larger auditors are more likely to give such opinions to their distressed clients. Overall, they address a deficiency in the literature relating to "the paucity of evidence on the value of auditor opinions to investors".

6

Trends in the Number of IPOs

Given the crucial role played by the IPO market in a country's financial and economic systems, many practitioners, academics, policy-makers, and the financial press have been alarmed at the prolonged drop in IPO activity that has characterized the recent years. Both the US and European markets have suffered from a decline in the number of companies going public. In the US, an annual average of 310 companies went public from 1980 to 2000, while this figure dropped to 99 during 2001–2012 (Gao et al., 2013), despite the doubling of the real gross domestic product during the entire period. Similarly, in Europe, an annual average of 293 companies went public from 1995 to 2000, while this number has dropped to 199 during 2001–2011 (Ritter et al., 2013). Since the 2000 technology bubble burst, IPO activity has not recovered to the pre-bubble levels. This section on IPO cycles explores the determining factors affecting a marked temporal fluctuation in the number of companies going public. In fact, 2005 seems to have breathed new life into the market compared to the small numbers of IPOs the Exchanges dealt in for several years after the Internet bubble burst. The question that has attracted scientific interest is therefore: what are the causes of the cycles that affect the number of IPOs?

The IPO market is highly cyclical. Historically, all world lists have had periods with a large number of IPO issues alternating with periods of sporadic downturns in issues. "Hot" IPO market periods occur when new IPOs are frequently issued, with these periods alternating with "cold" periods of very few new IPO issues.

The persistence of these phenomena and the recent Internet IPO bubble have drawn the academic world's attention to the cyclical nature of IPOs. The possible explanations proposed are based on three instances:

(a) the general economic conditions (business conditions);

(b) time-varying asymmetric information between the market and companies;

(c) investor sentiment.

In the first of these possible explanations, the intensity of issuances reflects the general economic conditions (Choe *et al.*, 1993; Fama and French, 1989): capital becomes available in a growing economy because profit expectations are high. The opportunity to access venture capital more easily persuades a larger number of companies to launch an IPO. On the other hand, it could be caused by an effect on demand: assuming that the cost of capital is stable, it is easier for companies to make profitable investments when economic conditions are generally good.

The second explanation refers to time-varying asymmetric information between the market and IPO issuing companies. When there are great levels of asymmetric information, investors ask for discounts on prices and this persuades companies to delay the IPO until better periods (Choe *et al.*, 1993). When asymmetric information decreases or is lacking, the number of IPOs increases: for example, after radical technological innovation which attracts a great deal of interest from the market and investors (Welch, 1989). Once the new technological innovations no longer interest all sectors to the same degree as they initially did, an increase in the number of IPOs only occurs in a few specific sectors. In fact, this idea is supported by evidence that hot issue periods are dominated by a large number of listings in a restricted number of sectors.

Lastly, an irrational explanation of the cyclical nature of IPOs according to investor sentiment is also possible (Loughran and Ritter, 1995). Periods in which investors are particularly optimistic are reflected in high demand for shares that in turn results in the cost of capital being lowered, therefore previously unprofitable investments become so. The pursuit of these new investment opportunities stimulates companies to access the markets and so the number of IPOs issued increases. Similarly, the variation in the number of IPOs can be interpreted as market inefficiency in that the volume of IPOs is high when shares are overvalued (Loughran and Ritter, 1995; Loughran et al., 1994). This assumption implies that the periods of mispricing can be recognized by the company controlling owners, who then launch an IPO, but not by investors.

While our discussion so far has synthesized the main reasons that may explain the cyclical trend in new listings, the remainder of the Section analyses the empirical verification for the three above reported reasons. It is noteworthy that empirical studies are not able to identify which and whether or not these possible explanations are the basis of the fluctuations in IPO numbers. In one of these studies, Lowry (2002) comes to conclusions coherent with reasons related to business conditions and investor sentiment. However, Ivanov and Lewis (2008) argue that the explanation of the fluctuations is not to be investigated on an aggregate level but by sector breakdown. As a result, while they confirm that business conditions and investor sentiment may explain the cyclical nature of manufacturing company IPOs, they do not apply to financial companies as the business conditions do not seem to play a relevant role. Then again, the situation affecting services is more complex and so the authors cannot empirically identify a plausible explanation.

Pastor and Veronesi (2005) model the time-clustering phenomenon of IPOs by considering the listing to be the exercise of an option by the entrepreneur-inventor. The entrepreneur, equipped with a business idea capable of generating excess profits, decides to float his own company when the market conditions are favorable. There is a positive correlation between the number of IPOs and market conditions, which are defined by previous market performance and price levels. In particular, the number of IPOs seems to be strongly correlated with the market performance during the previous six months, while the correlation with price level, measured by the ratio between market and book value, is weaker.

Lastly, a different point of view in the study of fluctuations in access to share markets lies in the role of the media. Indeed, the media can condition the market through their role of filtering and certifying information and therefore reducing the cost of access to relevant information. It can be hypothesized that investors might buy a larger number of shares if it is easier to find information about these shares. Falkenstein (1996) documents investment funds avoiding shares with little exposure in the media. In parallel, Barber and Odean (2005) provide direct evidence of the preference of individual investors to choose shares of companies that are "in the news". Moreover, the level of media exposure is reflected in improved liquidity and performance in the short-term (Antunovich and Sarkar, 2006). In terms of the launch of the IPO, the level of press coverage before the listing correlates positively with underpricing (DuCharme *et al.*, 2001; Ho *et al.*, 2001). *Vice versa*, greater underpricing in turn results in more mentions in the financial press, suggesting that underpricing publicizes the shares to investors who then buy them in the after-market (Demers and Lewellen, 2003). In particular, for American IPOs from 1996 to 2002 Bhattacharya *et al.* (2009) found that media exposure was greater for Internet-based companies and news about such companies was more positive than for non-Internet company IPOs during the bubble and more negative after the burst of the bubble.

7

Directions and Trends

In this monograph, we have summarized past and recent research on IPO-firms. We have tried to link entrepreneurship and finance literature to provide a systematic framework for analyzing the challenges and opportunities for entrepreneurial firms going public. We also highlighted topics that have been largely investigated by scholars, while pointing out themes that probably deserve more attention in the future.

From an entrepreneur's standpoint, staying private and obtaining capital through professional investors may be simpler and more desirable than going public: information released to the market can be limited and regulatory risks are lower. An IPO is expensive: investment bankers, lawyers, and auditors collectively charge millions of dollars to prepare the registration of the offering. This can be one of the reasons why the total number of companies listed in Europe and the US is much lower today[1] than during the 1990s. Moreover, the private capital market has grown aggressively, allowing emerging and technology companies to access more capital without going public. Recently, digital, disintermediated finance is also increasingly receiving attention. Disintermediated finance

---

[1]In 2018, 5,700 domestic companies were listed on exchanges in the European Union, while the US counted 4,397 companies. In 2008, numbers were 7,825 and 4,666 respectively. Source: World Federation of Exchanges.

allows entrepreneurial firms to raise funds directly from individual investors offline (business angels: refer to Edelman *et al.*, 2017 for a review of research on angel investing) or online from Internet users (e.g., crowdfunding) and seems suitable for financing entrepreneurial firms in their early stages, when firms are not yet attractive for venture capitalists and are not ready for an initial public offering (IPO).

Little is known about the effectiveness of disintermediated entrepreneurial finance in solving the financial constraints of entrepreneurial firms. By easing how demand for capital meets supply, the development of crowdfunding platforms is expected to improve the efficiency of financial markets (for a review of research on crowdfunding, refer to Wallmeroth *et al.*, 2018). However, the Internet has long presented the promise of entrepreneurial finance disintermediation, if not democratization. For example, in the 1990s, online auction IPOs were viewed as an alternative to the traditional book-building method of IPO underwriting and an efficient market mechanism to lower costs of going public (Ritter, 2013). Unfortunately, the expectations of online auction IPOs were never realized. Only one investment bank, W.R. Hambrecht, has developed a platform for online public offerings, and only 20 American companies, the most notable being Google, have gone public with online auctions (see Jay Ritter's IPOs Updated Statistics). The last auction IPO was held on May 25, 2007 (Clean Energy Fuels).

Further research is now required for new financing mechanisms. For instance, equity crowdfunding and initial coin offerings (ICOs) are to some extent replacing IPOs, in that they offer new opportunities to raise capital from a diversified set of investors. Similar to the way in which IPOs has made its way into the toolbox of entrepreneurs, equity crowdfunding offerings, ICOs and similar offerings have the potential to shape the entrepreneurial finance markets of the future (Block *et al.*, 2021). Johan and Zhang (2020) focus on information asymmetry between equity crowdfunding entrepreneurs and investors. Cumming *et al.* (2020) review different crowdfunding mechanisms in terms of whether achieving the funding goal is required for a successful offering. Cumming *et al.* (2021) compare IPOs and equity crowdfunding, pointing to some similarities in the structure of these two types of public equity offerings. Similarly, Huang *et al.* (2020) provide a comparison between ICOs and IPOs. Crowdfunding and ICOs involve raising funds from a large pool of backers (crowd) collected online by means of a web platform. These platforms will need to cope with collective-action problems, as crowd-investors have neither the ability nor the incentive, due to small investment sizes, to devote substantial resources to due diligence. Many of the traditional research questions in entrepreneurship and finance literature applied to IPOs could be reexamined in the crowdfunding and ICO context.

In the introduction, we argued that both IPOs and entrepreneurial ventures vary across "space and time". Like research on other topics, research on IPO companies follows a cycle, starting with the first waves on IPOs in the United States and Europe. This survey is less focused on the context but more on general findings which, we acknowledge, could not necessarily be generalized or treated as stylized facts. In the near future, IPOs as a means to finance fast growing entrepreneurial firms will likely be replaced/substituted by other forms of equity investment. At least, research should consider the potential of the new digital finance means of financing, where, unlike in the more traditional entrepreneurial finance segment of IPOs discussed in this monograph, the United States do not dominate. Some of the equity crowdfunding platforms with the largest transaction volume are based in Europe. This is partly due to regulatory effects. Although the Jumpstart Our Business Startups (JOBS) Act, which was signed into law on April 5, 2012, introduced crowdfunding as a means for entrepreneurs to raise equity financing in the United States, these markets were ultimately regulated by the SEC starting in 2015 and became effective on May 16, 2016. By contrast, equity crowdfunding developed in Europe in 2012. Overall, the empirical setting of most papers on equity crowdfunding is Europe. The evolution of research on this area is coherently likely to be less US-based relative to what has happened with IPOs.

References

Abrahamson, M., T. Jenkinson, and H. Jones (2011). "Why don't U.S. issuers demand European fees for IPOs?" *Journal of Finance*. 66(6): 2055–2082.

Acharya, V. and Z. Xu (2017). "Financial dependence and innovation: The case of public versus private firms". *Journal of Financial Economics*. 124(2): 223–243.

Aggarwal, R., S. Bhagat, and S. Rangan (2009). "The impact of fundamentals on IPO valuation". *Financial Management*. 38(2): 253–284.

Aggarwal, R., N. R. Prabhala, and M. Puri (2002). "Institutional allocation in initial public offerings: Empirical evidence". *Journal of Finance*. 57(3): 1421–1442.

Allen, F. and G. R. Faulhaber (1989). "Signaling by underpricing in the IPO market". *Journal of Financial Economics*. 23: 303–323.

Amihud, Y., S. Hauser, and A. Kirsch (2003). "Allocations, adverse selection and cascades in IPOs: Evidence from the Tel Aviv stock exchange". *Journal of Financial Economics*. 68: 137–158.

Anderson, C. W., J. Huang, and G. Torna (2017). "Can investors anticipate post-IPO mergers and acquisitions?" *Journal of Corporate Finance*. 45: 496–521.

Antunovich, P. and A. Sarkar (2006). "Fifteen minutes of fame? The market impact of internet stock picks". *Journal of Business.* 79(6): 3209–3232.

Arikan, A. M. and R. M. Stulz (2016). "Corporate acquisitions, diversification, and the firm's life cycle". *Journal of Finance.* 71(1): 139–194.

Arthurs, J. D., L. W. Busenitz, R. E. Hoskisson, and R. A. Johnson (2009). "Signaling and initial public offerings: The use and impact of the lockup period". *Journal of Business Venturing.* 24(4): 360–372.

Aslan, H. and P. Kumar (2011). "Lemons or cherries? Growth opportunities and market temptations in going public and private". *Journal of Financial and Quantitative Analysis.* 46(2): 489–526.

Audretsch, D. B. and E. E. Lehmann (2008). "The Neuer Markt as an institution of creation and destruction". *International Entrepreneurship and Management Journal.* 4(4): 419–429.

Audretsch, D. B. and E. E. Lehmann (2014). "Corporate governance and entrepreneurial firms". *Foundations and Trends® in Entrepreneurship.* 10(1–2): 1–160.

Ausubel, L. M. (2002). *Implications of auction theory for new issues markets.* Working Paper, University of Maryland.

Barber, B. M. and T. Odean (2005). *All that glitters: The effect of attention and news on the buying behavior of individual and institutional investors.* SSRN Working Paper.

Baron, D. P. (1982). "A model of the demand for investment bank advising and distribution services for new issues". *Journal of Finance.* 37: 955–976.

Benninga, S. and O. S. Helmantel (2005). "The timing of initial public offerings". *Journal of Financial Economics.* 75: 115–132.

Benson, D. F., J. C. Brau, J. Cicon, and S. P. Ferris (2015). "Strategically camouflaged corporate governance in IPOs: Entrepreneurial masking and impression management". *Journal of Business Venturing.* 30(6): 839–864.

Benveniste, L. and P. Spindt (1989). "How investment bankers determine the offer price and allocation of new issues". *Journal of Financial Economics.* 24: 343–361.

Berkman, H., M. E. Bradbury, and J. Ferguson (2000). "The accuracy of price-earnings and discounted cash flow methods of IPO equity valuation". *Journal of International Financial Management and Accounting.* 11(2): 71–83.

Bernstein, S. (2015). "Does going public affect innovation?" *The Journal of Finance.* 70: 1365–1403.

Bessembinder, H., J. Hao, and K. Zheng (2015). "Market making contracts, firm value, and the IPO decision". *The Journal of Finance.* 70: 1997–2028.

Bessler, W. and C. Bittelmeyer (2008). "Patents and the performance of technology firms: Evidence from initial public offerings in Germany". *Financial Markets and Portfolio Management.* 22(4): 323–356.

Bhattacharya, U., N. Galpin, R. Ray, and X. Yu (2009). "The role of the media in the Internet IPO bubble". *The Journal of Financial and Quantitative Analysis.* 44(3): 657–682.

Biais, B., P. Bossaerts, and J. C. Rochet (2002). "An optimal IPO mechanism". *Review of Economic Studies.* 69: 117–146.

Biais, B. and A. M. Faugeron-Crouzet (2002). "IPO auctions: English, dutch,. . .French and internet". *Journal of Financial Intermediation.* 11: 9–36.

Bikhchandani, S., D. Hirshleifer, and I. Welch (1992). "A theory of fads, fashion, custom, and cultural change as informational cascades". *Journal of Political Economy.* 100(5): 992–1026.

Bikhchandani, S., D. Hirshleifer, and I. Welch (1998). "Learning from the behavior of others: Conformity, fads, and informational cascades". *Journal of Economic Perspectives.* 12(3): 151–170.

Billings, M. and M. Lewis-Western (2016). "When does pre-IPO financial reporting trigger post-IPO legal consequences?" *Contemporary Accounting Research.* 33(1): 378–411.

Block, J., M. Colombo, D. Cumming, and S. Vismara (2018). "New players in entrepreneurial finance and why they are there". *Small Business Economics.* 50: 239–250.

Block, J. H., A. Groh, L. Hornuf, T. Vanacker, and S. Vismara (2021). "The entrepreneurial finance markets of the future: A comparison of crowdfunding and initial coin offerings". *Small Business Economics.* 57: 865–882.

Bodnaruk, A., E. Kandel, M. Massa, and A. Simonov (2008). "Shareholder diversification and the decision to go public". *The Review of Financial Studies*. 21(6): 2779–2824.

Boeh, K. K. and C. Dunbar (2016). "Underwriter deal pipeline and the pricing of IPOs". *Journal of Financial Economics*. 120(2): 383–399.

Boehmer, E. and R. Fishe (2001). *Who ends up short from underwriter short covering? A detailed analysis of IPO price stabilization.* Working Paper, University of Georgia and University of Miami.

Bonardo, D., S. Paleari, and S. Vismara (2011). "Valuing university-based firms: The effects of academic affiliation on IPO performance". *Entrepreneurship: Theory and Practice*. 35(4): 755–776.

Bonaventura, M. and G. Giudici (2017). "IPO valuation and profitability expectations: Evidence from the Italian exchange". *Eurasian Business Review*. 7(2): 247–266.

Bonaventura, M., G. Giudici, and S. Vismara (2018). "Valuation and performance of reallocated IPO shares". *Journal of International Financial Markets, Institutions and Money*. 54: 15–26.

Boot, A. W. A., R. Gopalan, and A. V. Thakor (2006). "The entrepreneur' choice between private and public ownership". *Journal of Finance*. 61: 803–836.

Boulton, T., S. Smart, and C. Zutter (2010). "IPO underpricing and international corporate governance". *Journal of International Business Studies*. 41: 206–222.

Boulton, T., S. Smart, and C. Zutter (2013). "Industrial diversification and underpricing of initial public offerings". *Financial Management*. 42(3): 679–704.

Boulton, T., S. Smart, and C. Zutter (2017). "Conservatism and international IPO underpricing". *Journal of International Business Studies*. 48(6): 763–785.

Brau, J. C., R. B. Couch, and N. K. Sutton (2012). "The desire to acquire and IPO long-run underperformance". *Journal of Financial and Quantitative Analysis*. 47(3): 493–510.

Brau, J. C. and S. E. Fawcett (2006). "Initial public offerings: An analysis of theory and practice". *Journal of Finance*. 61: 399–436.

Bruton, G. D., S. Chahine, and I. Filatotchev (2009). "Founders, private equity investors, and underpricing in entrepreneurial IPOs". *Entrepreneurship Theory and Practice.* 33: 909–923.

Bruton, G. D., I. Filatotchev, S. Chahine, and M. Wright (2010). "Governance, ownership structure, and performance of IPO firms: The impact of different types of private equity investors and institutional environments". *Strategic Management Journal.* 31: 491–509.

Bulow, J. and P. Klemperer (2002). "Prices and the winner's curse". *Rand Journal of Economics.* 33: 1–21.

Bustamante, M. C. (2012). "The dynamics of going public". *Review of Finance.* 16(2): 577–618.

Carpenter, R. and B. Petersen (2002). "Is the growth of small firms constrained by internal finance?" *Review of Economics and Statistics.* 84: 298–309.

Cassia, L., S. Paleari, and D. Vismara (2004). "The valuation of firms listed on the Nuovo Mercato: The peer comparables approach". *Advances in Financial Economics.* 10: 113–129.

Celikyurt, U., M. Sevilir, and A. Shivdasani (2010). "Going public to acquire? The acquisition motive in IPOs". *Journal of Financial Economics.* 96(3): 345–363.

Chahine, S., S. Saade, and M. Goergen (2019). "Foreign business activities, foreignness of the VC syndicate, and IPO value". *Entrepreneurship: Theory and Practice.* 43(5): 947–973.

Chaplinsky, S., K. W. Hanley, and S. K. Moon (2017). "The JOBS Act and the costs of going public". *Journal of Accounting Research.* 55: 795–836.

Chemmanur, T. J. (1993). "The pricing of initial public offerings: A dynamic model with information production". *Journal of Finance.* 48: 371–387.

Chemmanur, T. J. and J. He (2011). "IPO waves, product market competition, and the going public decision: Theory and evidence". *Journal of Financial Economics.* 101(2): 382–412.

Chemmanur, T. J., M. Gupta, and K. Simonyan (2020). "Top management team quality and innovation in venture-backed private firms and IPO market rewards to innovative activity". *Entrepreneurship: Theory and Practice.* Forthcoming.

Chen, J., C. S. Heng, B. C. Y. Tan, and Z. Lin (2018). "The distinct signaling effects of R&D subsidy and non-R&D subsidy on IPO performance of IT entrepreneurial firms in China". *Research Policy.* 47(1): 108–120.

Choe, H., R. W. Masulis, and V. Nanda (1993). "Common stock offerings across the business cycle". *Journal of Empirical Finance.* 1: 3–31.

Chou, T.-K., J.-C. Cheng, and C.-C. Chien (2013). "How useful is venture capital prestige? Evidence from IPO survivability". *Small Business Economics.* 40(4): 843–863.

Cogliati, G. M., S. Paleari, and S. Vismara (2011). "IPO pricing: Growth rates implied in offer prices". *Annals of Finance.* 7(1): 53–82.

Colombo, M. G., M. Meoli, and S. Vismara (2019). "Signaling in science-based IPOs: The combined effect of affiliation with prestigious universities, underwriters, and venture capitalists". *Journal of Business Venturing.* 34(1): 141–177.

Cumming, D. J., G. Leboeuf, and A. Schwienbacher (2020). "Crowdfunding models: Keep-it-all vs. all-or-nothing". *Financial Management.* 49(2): 331–360.

Cumming, D. J., M. Meoli, and S. Vismara (2021). "Does equity crowdfunding democratize entrepreneurial finance?" *Small Business Economics.* 56: 533–552.

Cumming, D. J. and S. Vismara (2017). "De-segmenting research in entrepreneurial finance". *Venture Capital.* 19(1–2): 17–27.

Daily, C. M., S. T. Certo, and D. R. Dalton (2005). "Investment bankers and IPO pricing: Does prospectus information matter?" *Journal of Business Venturing.* 20(1): 93–111.

Daily, C. M., S. T. Certo, D. R. Dalton, and R. Roengpitya (2003). "IPO underpricing: A meta-analysis and research synthesis". *Entrepreneurship Theory and Practice.* 27(3): 271–295.

Dalziel, T., R. J. Gentry, and M. Bowerman (2011). "An integrated agency-resource dependence view of the influence of directors' human and relational capital on firms' R&D spending". *Journal of Management Studies.* 48: 1217–1242.

Dambra, M., L. C. Field, and M. T. Gustafson (2015). "The JOBS Act and IPO volume: Evidence that disclosure costs affect the IPO decision". *Journal of Financial Economics.* 116(1): 121–143.

Deloof, M., W. De Maeseneire, and K. Inghelbrecht (2009). "How do investment banks value initial public offerings (IPOs)?" *Journal of Business Finance and Accounting.* 36(1–2): 130–160.

Demers, E. and P. Joos (2005). *IPO failure risk: Determinants and pricing consequences.* Working Paper, University of Rochester.

Demers, E. and K. Lewellen (2003). "The marketing role of IPOs: Evidence from internet stocks". *Journal of Financial Economics.* 68: 413–437.

Derrien, F. and K. Womack (2003). "Auctions vs. book-building and the control of underpricing in hot IPO markets". *Review of Financial Studies.* 16: 31–61.

DuCharme, L. L., S. Rajgopal, and S. Sefcik (2001). *Why was internet IPO underpricing so severe?* Working Paper, University of Washington.

Ecker, F. (2014). "Information precision and long-run performance of initial public offerings". *Contemporary Accounting Research.* 31: 876–910.

Edelman, L., T. Manolova, and C. Brush (2017). "Angel investing: A literature review". *Foundations and Trends® in Entrepreneurship.* 13(4–5): 265–439.

Ellingsen, T. and K. Rydqvist (1997). *The stock market as a screening device and the decision to go public.* Working Paper, Stockholm School of Economics and Norwegian School of Management.

Falkenstein, E. G. (1996). "Preferences for stock characteristics as revealed by mutual fund portfolio holdings". *Journal of Finance.* 51: 111–135.

Fama, E. F. (1998). "Market efficiency, long-term returns, and behavioral finance". *Journal of Financial Economics.* 49: 283–306.

Fama, E. F. and K. R. French (1989). "Business conditions and expected returns on stocks and bonds". *Journal of Financial Economics.* 25: 23–50.

Fama, E. F. and K. R. French (2004). "New lists: Fundamentals and survival rates". *Journal of Financial Economics.* 73: 229–269.

Fan, P. and K. Yamada (2020). "Same bed different dream composition of IPO shares and withdrawal decisions in weak market conditions". *Small Business Economics.* 55(4): 955–974.

Farag, H. and S. Johan (2021). "How alternative finance informs central themes in corporate finance". *Journal of Corporate Finance.* 67: 101879.

Ferris, S. P., Q. Hao, and M. Liao (2013). "The effect of issuer conservatism on IPO pricing and performance". *Review of Finance.* 17(3): 993–1027.

Field, L. C. and J. M. Karpoff (2002). "Takeover defenses of IPO firms". *Journal of Finance.* 57(5): 1857–1889.

Field, L. and M. Lowry (2009). "Institutional versus individual investment in IPOs: The importance of firm fundamentals". *The Journal of Financial and Quantitative Analysis.* 44(3): 489–516.

Friedlan, J. M. (1994). "Accounting choices of issuers of initial public offerings". *Contemporary Accounting Research.* 11(1): 1–31.

Gao, X., J. Ritter, and Z. Zhu (2013). "Where have all the IPOs gone?" *Journal of Financial and Quantitative Analysis.* 48(6): 1663–1692.

Giudici, G. and P. G. Roosenboom (2004). *The Rise and Fall of Europe's New Stock Markets, Advances in Financial Economics.* Emerald Publishing.

Gornall, W. and I. A. Strebulaev (2020). "Squaring venture capital valuations with reality". *Journal of Financial Economics.* 135(1): 120–143.

Hanley, K. and W. J. Wilhelm (1995). "Evidence on the strategic allocation of initial public offerings". *Journal of Financial Economics.* 37: 239–257.

Ho, B., M. Taher, R. Lee, and N. L. Fargher (2001). *Market sentiment, media hype and the underpricing of initial public offerings: The case of Australian technology IPOs.* Working Paper, University of New South Wales.

Holmström, B. and J. Tirole (1993). "Market liquidity and performance monitoring". *Journal of Political Economy.* 101: 678–709.

Houston, J., C. James, and J. Karceski (2006). "What a difference a month makes: Stock analyst valuations following initial public offerings". *Journal of Financial and Quantitative Analysis.* 41: 111–137.

Hovakimian, A. and I. Hutton (2010). "Merger-motivated IPOs". *Financial Management.* 39(4): 1547–1573.

How, J. C., K. Ngo, and P. Verhoeven (2011). "Dividend initiations and long-run IPO performance". *Australian Journal of Management.* 36(2): 267–286.

Hsieh, J., E. Lyandres, and A. Zhdanov (2011). "A theory of merger-driven IPOs". *Journal of Financial and Quantitative Analysis.* 46(5): 1367–1405.

Hsu, H.-C., A. V. Reed, and J. Rocholl (2010). "The new game in town: Competitive effects of IPOs". *The Journal of Finance.* 65: 495–528.

Huang, W., M. Meoli, and S. Vismara (2020). "The geography of initial coin offerings". *Small Business Economics.* 55: 77–102.

Hughes, P. J. and A. Thakor (1992). "Litigation risk, intermediation, and the underpricing of initial public offerings". *Review of Financial Studies.* 5: 709–742.

Huyghebaert, N. and C. Van Hulle (2006). "Structuring the IPO: Empirical evidence on the portions of primary and secondary shares". *Journal of Corporate Finance.* 12: 296–320.

Ibbotson, R. G. (1975). "Price performance of common stock new issues". *Journal of Financial Economics.* 2: 235–272.

Ivanov, V. and C. M. Lewis (2008). "The determinants of market-wide issue cycles for initial public offerings". *Journal of Corporate Finance.* 14(5): 567–583.

Jagannathan, R. and A. Sherman (2006). *Why do IPO auctions fail?* Working Paper, Northwestern University.

Jain, B. A. and O. Kini (1994). "The post-issue operating performance of IPO firms". *Journal of Finance.* 49: 1699–1726.

Jain, B. A. and O. Kini (2004). *Industry investment conditions, strategic investment choices, and the post-issue operating performance of IPO firms.* Working Paper, Georgia State University.

Jain, B. A., N. Jayaraman, and O. Kini (2008). "The path-to-profitability of Internet IPO firms". *Journal of Business Venturing.* 23(2): 165–194.

Jain, B. A. and F. Tabak (2008). "Factors influencing the choice between founder versus non-founder CEOs for IPO firms". *Journal of Business Venturing.* 23(1): 21–45.

Jaskiewicz, P., V. M. González, S. Menéndez, and D. Schiereck (2005). "Long-run IPO performance analysis of German and Spanish family-owned businesses". *Family Business Review*. 18(3): 179–202.

Jenkinson, T., A. D. Morrison, and W. J. Wilhelm (2006). "Why are European IPOs so rarely priced outside the indicative price range?" *Journal of Financial Economics*. 80: 185–209.

Jensen, M. C. and W. Meckling (1976). "Theory of the firm managerial behavior, agency costs and ownership structures". *Journal of Financial Economics*. 3: 305–360.

Jia, M. and Z. Zhang (2014). "Corporate philanthropy and IPOs". *Journal of Management Studies*. 51: 1118–1152.

Johan, S. and Y. Zhang (2020). "Quality revealing versus overstating in equity crowdfunding". *Journal of Corporate Finance*. 65: 101741.

Judge, W. Q., M. A. Witt, A. Zattoni, T. Talaulicar, J. J. Chen, K. Lewellyn, H. W. Hu, D. Shukla, R. G. Bell, J. Gabrielsson, F. Lopez, S. Yamak, Y. Fassin, D. McCarthy, J. L. Rivas, S. Fainshmidt, and H. Van Ees (2015). "Corporate governance and IPO underpricing in a cross-national sample: A multilevel knowledge-based view". *Strategic Management Journal*. 36: 1174–1185.

Kahneman, D. and A. Tversky (1982). "The simulation heuristic". In: *Judgement Under Uncertainty: Heuristics and Biases*. Ed. by D. Kahneman, P. Slovic, and A. Tversky. New York: Cambridge University Press. 201–208.

Kaplan, S. N. and R. S. Ruback (1995). "The valuation of cash flow forecasts: An empirical analysis". *Journal of Finance*. 50: 1059–1093.

Kaur, A. and B. Singh (2015). "Does gender diversity on Indian boards impede IPO underpricing?" *Management and Labour Studies*. 40(1–2): 194–205.

Khoury, T. A., M. Junkunc, and D. L. Deeds (2013). "The social construction of legitimacy through signaling social capital: Exploring the conditional value of alliances and underwriters at IPO". *Entrepreneurship: Theory and Practice*. 37(3): 569–601.

Khurshed, A., S. Paleari, and S. Vismara (2003). *The operating performance of initial public offerings: The UK experience*. SSRN Working Paper.

Khurshed, A., S. Paleari, A. Pande, and S. Vismara (2014). "Transparent bookbuilding, certification and initial public offerings". *Journal of Financial Markets*. 19: 154–169.

Kim, M. and J. R. Ritter (1999). "Valuing IPOs". *Journal of Financial Economics*. 53(3): 409–437.

Kolb, J. and T. Tykvová (2016). "Going public via special purpose acquisition companies: Frogs do not turn into princes". *Journal of Corporate Finance*. 40: 80–96.

Krishnan, C., V. Ivanov, R. Masulis, and A. Singh (2011). "Venture capital reputation, post-IPO performance, and corporate governance". *Journal of Financial and Quantitative Analysis*. 46(5): 1295–1333.

Kroll, M., B. Walters, and S. Le (2007). "The impact of board composition and top management team ownership structure on post-IPO performance in young entrepreneurial firms". *The Academy of Management Journal*. 50(5): 1198–1216.

Lee, S. H., S. B. Bach, and Y. S. Baik (2011). "The impact of IPOs on the values of directly competing incumbents". *Strategic Entrepreneurship Journal*. 5(2): 158–177.

Lehmann, E. E. and S. Vismara (2020). "Corporate governance in IPO firms". *Annals of Corporate Governance*. 5(1): 1–100.

Leitterstorf, M. P. and S. B. Rau (2014). "Socioemotional wealth and IPO underpricing of family firms". *Strategic Management Journal*. 35: 751–760.

Leland, H. and D. Pyle (1977). "Informational asymmetries, financial structure, and financial intermediation". *Journal of Finance*. 32: 371–387.

Levis, M. and S. Vismara (2013). *Handbook of Research on IPO*. Cheltenham: Edward Elgar.

Li, O. Z., Y. Lin, and J. R. Robinson (2016). "The effect of capital gains taxes on the initial pricing and underpricing of IPOs". *Journal of Accounting and Economics*. 61(2–3): 465–485.

Liu, K., J. D. Arthurs, D. Nam, and F.-T. Mousa (2014a). "Information diffusion and value redistribution among transaction partners of the IPO firm". *Strategic Management Journal*. 35: 1717–1726.

Liu, L., A. Sherman, and Y. Zhang (2014b). "The long-run role of the media: Evidence from initial public offerings". *Management Science.* 60(8): 1945–1964.

Ljungqvist, A. (2009). "IPO underpricing: A survey". In: *Handbook of Corporate Finance: Empirical Corporate Finance.* Ed. by B. Espen Eckbo. Elsevier.

Ljungqvist, A. and W. J. Wilhelm (2002). "IPO allocations: Discriminatory or discretionary?" *Journal of Financial Economics.* 65: 167–201.

Loughran, T. and J. Ritter (1995). "The new issues puzzle". *Journal of Finance.* 50: 23–51.

Loughran, T., J. Ritter, and K. Rydqvist (1994). "Initial public offerings: International insights". *Pacific-Basin Finance Journal.* 2: 165–199.

Lowry, M. (2002). "Why does IPO volume fluctuate so much?" *Journal of Financial Economics.* 67: 3–41.

Lowry, M., R. Michaely, and E. Volkova (2017). "Initial public offerings: A synthesis of the literature and directions for future research". *Foundations and Trends® in Finance.* 11(3–4): 154–320.

Lowry, M. and K. J. Murphy (2007). "Executive stock options and IPO underpricing". *Journal of Financial Economics.* 85(1): 39–65.

Maksimovic, V. and P. Pichler (2001). "Technological innovation and initial public offerings". *Review of Financial Studies.* 14: 459–494.

Manigart, S. and M. Wright (2013). "Venture capital investors and portfolio firms". *Foundations and Trends® in Entrepreneurship.* 9(4–5): 365–570.

Mello, A. S. and J. E. Parsons (1998). "Going public and the ownership structure of the firm". *Journal of Financial Economics.* 49: 79–109.

Meoli, M., S. Paleari, and S. Vismara (2013). "Completing the technology transfer process: M&As of science-based IPOs". *Small Business Economics.* 40(2): 227–248.

Michel, J.-S. (2014). "Return on recent VC investment and long-run IPO returns". *Entrepreneurship: Theory and Practice.* 38(3): 527–549.

Modigliani, F. M. and H. Miller (1958). "The cost of capital, corporation finance, and the theory of investment". *American Economic Review.* 48: 261–297.

Moore, C. B., R. G. Bell, and I. Filatotchev (2010). "Institutions and foreign IPO firms: The effects of 'home' and 'host' country institutions on performance". *Entrepreneurship Theory and Practice*. 34(3): 469–490.

Morricone, S., F. Munari, R. Oriani, and G. de Rassenfosse (2017). "Commercialization strategy and IPO underpricing". *Research Policy*. 46(6): 1133–1141.

Mousa, F. and R. Reed (2013). "The impact of slack resources on high-tech IPOs". *Entrepreneurship Theory and Practice*. 37(5): 1123–1147.

Mumi, A., M. Obal, and Y. Yang (2019). "Investigating social media as a firm's signaling strategy through an IPO". *Small Business Economics*. 53(3): 631–645.

Nagata, K. and T. Hachiya (2007). "Earnings management and the pricing of initial public offerings". *Review of Pacific Basin Financial Markets and Policies*. 10(4): 541–559.

Pagano, M. (1993). "Financial markets and growth: An overview". *European Economic Review*. 37(2–3): 613–622.

Pagano, M., A. Panetta, and L. Zingales (1998). "Why do companies go public? An empirical analysis". *Journal of Finance*. 53: 27–64.

Paleari, S., A. Signori, and S. Vismara (2014). "How do underwriters select peers when valuing IPOs?" *Financial Management*. 43(4): 731–755.

Pandya, F. H. (2016). "After market pricing performance of initial public offerings (IPOs)". *Jindal Journal of Business Research*. 5(1): 1–16.

Park, H. D. and P. C. Patel (2015). "How does ambiguity influence IPO underpricing? The role of the signalling environment". *Journal of Management Studies*. 52: 796–818.

Pastor, L. and P. Veronesi (2005). "Rational IPO waves". *Journal of Finance*. 60: 1713–1757.

Peristiani, S. and G. Hong (2004). *Pre-IPO Financial Performance and Aftermarket Survival, Current Issues 10*. Federal Reserve Bank of New York.

Planell, S. B. (1995). *Determinantes y efectos de la salida a bolsa en España: Un analisi empirico.* Working Paper, Centro de Estudios Monetarios y Financieros, Spain.

Purnanandam, A. K. and B. Swaminathan (2004). "Are IPOs really underpriced?" *The Review of Financial Studies.* 17(3): 811–848.

Ragozzino, R. and J. J. Reuer (2007). "Initial public offerings and the acquisition of entrepreneurial firms". *Strategic Organization.* 5(2): 155–176.

Ragozzino, R. and J. J. Reuer (2011). "Geographic distance and corporate acquisitions: Signals from IPO firms". *Strategic Management Journal.* 32(8): 876–894.

Reuer, J. J., T. W. Tong, and C. Wu (2012). "A signaling theory of acquisition premiums: Evidence from IPO targets". *Academy of Management Journal.* 55: 667–683.

Ritter, J. R. (1987). "The costs of going public". *Journal of Financial Economics.* 19(2): 269–281.

Ritter, J. R. (1991). "The long-run performance of initial public offerings". *Journal of Finance.* 46: 3–27.

Ritter, J. R. (2013). "Re-energizing the IPO market". In: *Restructuring to Speed Economic Recovery.* Ed. by M. N. Bailey, R. J. Herring, and Y. Seki. Washington: Brookings Press.

Ritter, J. R. and I. Welch (2002). "A review of IPO activity, pricing, and allocations". *Journal of Finance.* 57: 1795–1828.

Ritter, J. R., A. Signori, and S. Vismara (2013). "Economies of scope and IPO activity in Europe". In: *Handbook of Research on IPOs.* Ed. by M. Levis and S. Vismara. Cheltenham, UK: Edward Elgar Publishing. 11–34.

Rocholl, J. (2005). *The private benefits of listing.* SSRN Working Paper.

Rock, K. (1986). "Why new issues are underpriced". *Journal of Financial Economics.* 15: 187–212.

Roosenboom, P. G. J. (2007). "How do underwriters value initial public offerings? An empirical analysis of the French IPO market". *Contemporary Accounting Research.* 24(4): 1217–1243.

Roosenboom, P. G. J. (2012). "Valuing and pricing IPOs". *Journal of Banking and Finance.* 36(6): 1653–1664.

Rydqvist, K. and K. Högholm (1995). "Going public in the 1980s: Evidence from Sweden". *European Financial Management*. 1: 287–315.

Sanders, W. M. G. and S. T. Boivie (2004). "Sorting things out: Valuation of new firms in uncertain markets". *Strategic Management Journal*. 25: 167–186.

Schenone, C. (2004). "The effect of banking relations on the firm's IPO underpricing". *Journal of Finance*. 59: 2903–2958.

Schultz, P. and M. Zaman (2001). "Do the individuals closest to Internet firms believe they are overvalued". *Journal of Financial Economics*. 59: 347–381.

Sherman, A. (2005). "Global trends in IPO methods: Book building versus auctions with endogenous entry". *Journal of Financial Economics*. 78(3): 615–649.

Sherman, A. and S. Titman (2002). "Building the IPO order book: Underpricing and participation limits with costly information". *Journal of Financial Economics*. 65: 3–29.

Signori, A. and S. T. Vismara (2017). "Stock-financed M&As of newly listed firms". *Small Business Economics*. 48(1): 115–134.

Signori, A. and S. Vismara (2018). "M&A synergies and trends in IPOs". *Technological Forecasting and Social Change*. 127: 141–153.

Smart, S. B., R. S. Thirumalai, and C. J. Zutter (2008). "What's in a vote? The short- and long-run impact of dual-class equity on IPO firm values". *Journal of Accounting and Economics*. 45(1): 94–115.

Stoughton, N. M. and J. Zechner (1998). "IPO-mechanisms, monitoring and ownership structure". *Journal of Financial Economics*. 49: 45–77.

Sundaramurthy, C., K. Pukthuanthong, and Y. Kor (2014). "Positive and negative synergies between the CEO's and the corporate board's human and social capital: A study of biotechnology firms". *Strategic Management Journal*. 35: 845–868.

Teoh, S. H., I. Welch, and T. J. Wong (1998). "Earnings management and the long-run market performance of initial public offerings". *Journal of Finance*. 53: 1935–1974.

Thaler, R. (1980). "Towards a positive theory of consumer choice". *Journal of Economic Behavior and Organization*. 1: 39–60.

Tinic, S. M. (1988). "Anatomy of initial public offerings of common stocks". *The Journal of Finance*. 18: 789–822.

Tversky, A. and D. Kahneman (1981). "The framing of decisions and psychology of choice". *Science*. 211: 453–458.

Useche, D. (2014). "Are patents signals for the IPO market? An EU-US comparison for the software industry". *Research Policy*. 43(8): 1299–1311.

Vismara, S. (2018). "Information cascades among investors in equity crowdfunding". *Entrepreneurship Theory and Practice*. 42(3): 467–497.

Vismara, S., S. Paleari, and J. R. Ritter (2012). "Europe's second markets for small companies". *European Financial Management*. 18(3): 352–388.

Vismara, S., A. Signori, and S. Paleari (2015). "Changes in underwriters' selection of comparable firms pre- and post-IPO: Same bank, same company, different peer". *Journal of Corporate Finance*. 34: 235–250.

Wagner, S. and I. Cockburn (2010). "Patents and the survival of Internet-related IPOs". *Research Policy*. 39(2): 214–228.

Wallmeroth, J., P. Wirtz, and A. Groh (2018). "Venture capital, angel financing, and crowdfunding of entrepreneurial ventures: A literature review". *Foundations and Trends® in Entrepreneurship*. 14(1): 1–129.

Wang, X. and P. Wan (2013). "Explaining the variance in underpricing among VC-backed IPOs". *Strategic Entrepreneurship Journal*. 7: 331–342.

Weber, J. and M. Willenborg (2003). "Do expert informational intermediaries add value? Evidence from auditors in microcap initial public offerings". *Journal of Accounting Research*. 41: 681–720.

Welch, I. (1989). "Seasoned offerings, imitation costs, and the underpricing of initial public offerings". *Journal of Finance*. 44: 421–450.

Welch, I. (1992). "Sequential sales, learning, and cascades". *Journal of Finance*. 47: 695–732.

Wilhelm, W. J. (2005). "Bookbuilding, auctions, and the future of the IPO process". *Journal of Applied Corporate Finance*. 17: 55–66.

Willenborg, M., B. Wu, and Y. S. Yang (2015). "Issuer operating performance and IPO price formation". *Journal of Accounting Research.* 53: 1109–1149.

Wu, G. A. (2012). "The effect of going public on innovative productivity and exploratory search". *Organization Science.* 23(4): 928–950.

Yang, Q., M. Zimmerman, and C. Jiang (2011). "An empirical study of the impact of CEO characteristics on new firms' time to IPO". *Journal of Small Business Management.* 49(2): 163–184.

Zheng, S. X. (2007). "Are IPOs really overpriced?" *Journal of Empirical Finance.* 14(3): 287–309.

Zingales, L. (1995). "Insider ownership and the decision to go public". *Review of Economic Studies.* 60: 425–448.